SJSU SAN JOSÉ STATE UNIVERSITY

Dear Students,

Welcome to San José State University!

We are very pleased that you will be joining the Spartan family this fall. Our goal as a university is to help you complete your degree in four years and depart with the skills and knowledge you need to be successful in your life and career.

As you prepare for your first semester on campus, we are delighted to provide you with a copy of our 2017-18 Campus Reading Program selection, *Hot Dogs and Hamburgers* by Rob Shindler. Each summer, our campus community is invited to participate in reading and discussing a common book. Discussions and other activities take place throughout the semester bringing together students, professors and staff members to talk about the selected book. These activities give you an opportunity to engage in college-level discourse while creating new personal connections with fellow Spartans that will support you long after graduation.

We hope you view this reading opportunity as an enjoyable first "assignment" and as a way to help you orient to life in college.

Shindler's memoir, about his experience helping his son overcome learning disabilities and working as an adult literacy tutor, is an especially fitting selection for us. The book explores the importance of lifelong learning—in and out of the classroom—while also sharing the ways volunteering can enrich our lives. San José State is uniquely committed to providing opportunities to participate in service learning projects in our community. We believe community "experiential learning" enhances the quality of life in our region and enables you to put what you learn in the classroom to practical use.

You can learn about these fall activities, discussion groups and guided study materials for this text, and more at http://www.sjsu.edu/reading/. The book is available in alternate formats upon request; please contact the Accessible Education Center at (408) 924-6000 for assistance.

Our top priority is your success, and we are glad you have chosen San José State to fulfill your dreams of a four-year college degree. We look forward to welcoming you to campus this fall!

Sincerely,

Mary A. Papazian
President
San José State University

Andy Feinstein
Provost and Senior VP for Academic Affairs
San José State University

HOT DOGS & HAMBURGERS

Unlocking Life's Potential by Inspiring Literacy at Any Age

ROB SHINDLER

RIVER GROVE BOOKS

The names and identifying characteristics of persons referenced in this book, as well as identifying events and places, may have been changed to protect the privacy of the individuals and their families.

Published by River Grove Books
Austin, TX
www.greenleafbookgroup.com

Distributed by River Grove Books
For ordering information or special discounts for bulk purchases, please contact River Grove Books at PO Box 91869, Austin, TX 78709, 512.891.6100.

Design and composition by Greenleaf Book Group LLC
Cover design by Greenleaf Book Group LLC
Cover photo: ©iStockphoto.com/Stanislav Pobytov

Publisher's Cataloging-In-Publication Data
(Prepared by The Donohue Group, Inc.)

Shindler, Rob.
Hot dogs & hamburgers : unlocking life's potential by inspiring literacy at any age / Rob Shindler.—1st ed.
p. ; cm.
Issued also as an ebook.
Includes bibliographical references.
1. Shindler, Rob. 2. Functional literacy—United States. 3. Tutors and tutoring—United States. 4. Learning disabled children—United States. 5. Parents of children with disabilities—United States. I. Title. II. Title: Hot dogs and hamburgers
LC151 .S55 2012
372.6 2012944366

ISBN: 978-1-63299-149-2

Other Editions
First Edition ISBN: 978-1-938416-09-5
Ebook ISBN: 978-1-938416-10-1

Custom Edition

To my wife, Andi, who always makes me feel like the most important person in the room, even when I'm not.

I only have an hour, only sixty minutes in it. Forced upon me, can't refuse it. Didn't seek it, didn't choose it. But it's up to me to use it. Give account if I abuse it. Just a tiny little hour. But eternity is in it.

—Anonymous

PROLOGUE

SPECIAL ED are not exactly the two words you think about when you're picking out cribs and playpens. Fathers' future hopes for their kids begin the first moment they know they want to be a dad. I was devastated to discover that my offspring, my son, wasn't perfect. And unlike a captain who stands strong when his ship unexpectedly sails off course, I temporarily abandoned my first mate. But that's not where my story starts and my journey begins.

I lived at home with my parents until I was thirty—thirty-one, if we're giving out brownie points for honesty. I'd still be sleeping on my Batman & Robin sheets if Princess Andi hadn't rescued me. She turned me into a man. It was Oliver, however, who made me a dad.

After getting married, Andi and I moved into our dream house, ready to start a family. The house sat right behind a beautiful park with swings, monkey bars, and teeter-totters. A week after unpacking, we discovered we couldn't make a baby. So began our climb up and down the ladder of infertility. After years filled with shots and prayers, potions and lotions—not to mention the hundreds of vacant ultrasound screens we stared at downheartedly—we finally struck gold. Twice. With the help of our fertility specialist (and God), we made our twins, Isabella and Oliver.

After they started school, we were told that Oliver had a severe learning disability. Although I knew how to entertain my children by making the funny noise with my hand under my armpit, I gave up on trying to help my son, and I let everyone else carry the load. Eventually, however, I found my son's dad. By discovering a way to teach adult strangers, I found the road to helping my own little boy.

The common perception about learning issues and adult illiteracy is that somehow they're reserved for a certain group of people. In other words, uneducated, lazy, apathetic minorities. I know now, firsthand, how ridiculous this theory is. Over the last few years, I have been surrounded by ambitious people who are eloquent, driven, clever, and funny enough to make you laugh out loud. They couldn't read, but they wanted to become better.

My hope is that our story will show readers that literacy issues reside in all neighborhoods and that the victims of illiteracy can find dignity and life's possibilities by learning to read.

CHAPTER 1

I'm waiting for the elevator to arrive. Even though it's the middle of the day, the lobby of this busy metropolitan building is completely empty. Finally the bell dings, the doors open, and I step inside. After pressing number nine, I notice my shoelace is undone, so I kneel down to tie it. Before the steel doors close, a hand pokes its way in and prevents them from shutting. Actually, it's more like a paw—of a grizzly bear. Its fingers resemble five frozen bananas dipped in chocolate sauce. I gaze at the owner of that paw as he steps inside to join me. I feel as though I'm looking up at the character Jack discovered when he reached the top of the beanstalk.

I wonder if this man is wondering why I hadn't held the door for him. As we climb upward, I realize he may be bigger than a grizzly bear. I also can't help noticing he has yet to select his own floor. While waiting downstairs in the lobby, I had glanced at the directory of the different businesses and establishments in the building. I reviewed them now as the elevator began its climb. The Department of Transportation has two offices, one on the tenth floor and the other on the twelfth. There's a massage school on the fifth, a real estate school on the seventh, and a travel agency on the eighth. You can become a hair stylist by pressing three, and you can learn to make a wicked Long Island Iced Tea stepping off on six.

As we ride together in silence, I can't stop looking at my traveling companion's nails. They're the size of postage stamps. I'm forty-five, and the top of my head barely reaches the zipper on his light brown United Parcel Service jacket.

Normally, it would be quite comforting to know this elevator had been tested and properly maintained just fourteen short months ago by Earl T. Wilkens. But with Bigfoot standing next to me, I'm not so sure I'm safe. He could finish me for lunch before hunting for dinner. Please don't break down now, I pray.

Elevators are funny little cubed places. You can choose to be alone in these motorized squares even when sharing intimate space with complete strangers who are standing closer to one another than they've stood among relatives in their own family. You can say hello, good-bye, or nothing at all. You can be a stand-up comic, a philosopher, a weatherman, or a tour guide. I've cried in elevators. I've practiced closing arguments inside them. I've daydreamed. As I've mentioned, I've prayed.

Elevators are also like shadow boxes holding special memories from different chapters of our lives. I remember my very first elevator ride. I was about seven years old and I was shopping with my mom at Marshall Fields. I put on my fancy dress clothes and we rode the train to downtown Chicago. It was so exciting to push all the buttons. Even though back then they didn't light up, it was still pretty powerful to believe I could control the elevator. I loved it being just my mom and me inside there together.

I also remember the night I went to pick up Andi for our first date. I was so nervous I rode up and down to the fifteenth floor three separate times.

Years later, I remember riding the elevator down together moments after our wedding. How beautiful she looked in those mirrored steel doors and how her gown and train filled the compartment. I also remember riding the elevator up for our first appointment to see the infertility specialist. Both so nervous, neither speaking a word but knowing exactly what the other was thinking. And a few years later, the feeling of joy as we descended from the maternity ward at Northwestern Hospital with our two-day-old twins, ready to step outside to begin our new life together as a family.

As the doors finally open at the ninth floor, I step out and walk toward the sign on the wall that says Literacy Chicago. I stop at the desk to sign in. It's three fifty and my tutoring career begins in ten minutes. I decide to make a quick visit to the restroom. I return to the classroom, take a seat at the desk, and nervously open my *Tutor's Handbook*. I'm so nervous, in fact, I don't even notice him sitting in front of me. I lift my head and he nods hello. And then he smiles. A smile that certainly could never eat anyone for lunch. Or dinner. The kind of smile you remember when you need to be reminded of what a smile should look like.

He no longer seems dangerous. And his giant hands are folded politely in his lap. Before, when we stood together in the elevator, I saw him as a person who could harm me, probably how everyone else views him. But in this room, he's just a UPS guy who wants to learn how to read. As I get up and approach him, he looks into my eyes the way you teach your son to look at someone when he meets the person for the first time. "Hi, I'm Melvin," he says and holds out his hand. As we shake, he continues speaking. "Thank you for coming here today and for being my tutor."

I realize at that moment I had done something else during our ride in the elevator. I had judged a book by its cover.

CHAPTER 2

That early tutoring session with Melvin was a world away—in a field of dreams, you could say—from when I initially learned about my own son's reading deficiencies.

At first, we dads and moms on the sideline think the two boys on the field are only chatting. But then I realize it's not just simple teammate banter about grabbing a milkshake together after the game. They're arguing, and Oliver—standing on third base—keeps turning his head back and forth jerkily like a robot with a mechanical tick. I can see his mouth moving ferociously up and down, but I can't make out what he's saying because I'm sitting too far away behind the fence with the other parents. Every time Oliver turns toward home plate, I can see those oversized gums of his. They're a little too big for his mouth: his teeth should start here, but instead they start there. During any normal conversation you can't help but see Oliver's prominent gums. You particularly notice them when he's smiling or laughing. At the moment, he's doing neither, because now these two eleven-year-olds of the Wells Park Junior Orioles are tangled up in a knock-down, drag-out debate about which one gets to throw the practice ball back into the dugout before the inning begins.

Silly to most, this verbal battle is life altering for two Little Leaguers. And then, coming out of left field, literally, Jordan yells, "Yeah, well at least I'm not in special ed, retard." And suddenly I witness all the spirit and self-confidence disappear from Oliver's body. He deflates in front of my—our—eyes, standing next to third base with his head hanging giraffe low to the ground, craving a hole he can climb into.

As I ached for my son, a flood of memories washed through my mind. The conversation I'd had a few years before Oliver was born, for instance, with a friend of mine who shared a very intimate story. The kind of story men don't traditionally volunteer unless multiple cocktails are involved. After learning that his son was severely autistic, he confessed, it was as if he had suffered a sudden death. An assassination of all the hopes and dreams he had held since the moment he first knew his wife was pregnant. With a Boy. He mourned the loss of what would never be: Peewee Quarterback. Eighth-Grade Class President. High School Prom King. Youthful conquests slipping away before his son had even had his first visit from the Tooth Fairy.

And I thought of my own response to the news about Oliver's difficulty in school. In *Webster's*, the word *disappear* is defined as vanishing from sight. To cease to exist. That's exactly what I did when I first found out about my son's situation. That's what Miss Jennifer called it. His "situation." His "learning disability." Are you out of your mind? I said to myself. That stuff happens to other people. People whose kids ride on short little yellow buses and eat paste right out of the can. (As if eating it from a paper plate or in some other respectable fashion would be any less disturbing.)

I was never embarrassed by or because of Oliver. I was scared for him. Or maybe I was just scared for myself. I'm not sure what drove my fear, but early on I did my best to guard this private information from becoming public knowledge. I never wanted people treating my son differently. I knew how cruel society, especially kids, can be, and I didn't want anyone reaching quick verdicts before all the evidence was in.

It was a few weeks after the twins entered Lakeshore Preparatory Academy when Miss Jennifer first noticed Oliver wasn't learning as quickly as the rest of his preschool mates. As I sat there quietly during our first parent-teacher conference, my blood began to boil: What kind of name is Lakeshore Preparatory Academy, anyway? These youngsters are five freaking years old, for God's sake. What could the teachers be preparing them for, pudding and a nap?

Miss Jennifer elaborated on Oliver's situation, saying he was deficient in his processing skills and was having difficulty with the alphabet and pronouncing the sounds of almost every single one of its twenty-six letters. Poor Miss Jennifer. She didn't nearly deserve all the remarks I made about her behind her back. And in our kitchen. And in the bedroom. And in the garage. Oliver was my little boy and he could be anything he wanted to be in this world. So what if he had some trouble pronouncing some of the letters in the alphabet? That didn't mean he had a "situation." A situation is having a third ear, not having problems with the letter G.

Over the next few years, I may have remained physically present in Oliver's life, but I stayed as far away as possible from dealing with his learning struggles. I was walking around wearing dark-colored glasses of denial, refusing to consider the possibility that Oliver could have a serious problem with reading. My refusal to accept the assessments concerning my son also affected the most precious relationship I have. Although Isabella and Oliver may have been too young to notice their father's inadequacies, Andi wasn't. You envision your partner being a cheerleader for your children, not a spectator. I became emotionally and spiritually invisible. I allowed everybody else to carry his educational load: That meant his mother, the revolving door of weekly tutors, and the special education department at Walter J. Newberry Academy, the grammar school he attended after graduating from Lakeshore.

Oliver began his education at Newberry as a kindergartner, at which point he immediately took a seat in the second row of Miss McLain's classroom. Miss McLain had recently graduated from a small teaching college in Lincoln, Nebraska, and had become the special education teacher at Newberry. "Warden of the Misfits," as some cruel upperclassmen referred to the teacher in Room 208. Misfits, by the way, is just one of the words flung around to describe kids with special needs. Others we've heard over the years include retard, stupid, idiot, moron, dumb, and the ever-popular loser.

Loser? Oliver's not the loser. I am. What kind of father turns his back on his own son? That's not a question; it's a confession. As I've just shared, I let my own fear and my own insecurity about not producing the perfect offspring drive me into neutral. I was a parent stuck in quicksand, incapable of performing the most basic of parental acts: being there unconditionally and completely for my kid. Thankfully, at the time, Oliver was too young to fully comprehend the chinks in my armor. Armor held together with mirrors and Silly Putty.

I did make one futile attempt at grabbing the bull by the horns, though, when Oliver was about six years old. It was right after we met with the child psychologist Miss Jennifer referred us to.

I humored the "kid shrink" as we sat frozen on her twenty-thousand-dollar couch listening to her hand down the official diagnosis dressed up with some fancy verbs, codes, and numbers. Judith (she insisted on us using her first name) spoke of the years in special education Oliver would need just to make it past grammar school. I felt like Andi and I were trapped inside a pack of Starbursts. Every wall in the office was a different color: oranges and limes and strawberries and grapes.

After our session with Judy, I lay back in my sugar-induced coma gazing up at her wall of fame with its baker's dozen of degrees while she put Oliver through a battery of tests. He wore a pair of oversized headphones and raised his hand every time a certain sound chimed. As Oliver took off the headphones and gave them to the technician, he looked over at me. Holding his thumb in the air, he said, "See, Daddy, I'm not deaf."

Dr. J's official diagnosis was that our son exhibited a receptive/expressive language disorder characterized by significantly reduced comprehension and processing skills, as well as an articulator/phonological/neurological disorder presenting deficits that would have a significant impact in his language function. Truthfully, I liked Miss Jennifer's "situation" explanation a whole lot better!

After stepping off the elevator that day and walking toward the car clenching Andi's moist hand and Oliver's chubby one, I was determined to cure the problem on my own. My plan was simple. I'd attack the alphabet a letter at a time. One a night, times twenty-six letters, equals twenty-six nights. I'd have this articulator thingamajig solved in less than a month.

I decide to set up a workshop for me and my pal Oliver inside my bedroom closet. I know I have to find someplace quiet and private so he will be hundreds of feet away from SpongeBob SquarePants and the rest of his adopted cartoon family. I write out each letter on a separate note card in a different color. As a pre-tutorial treat, I bring up two slices of blueberry pie with a side of chocolate ice cream for each of us. Our man cave, our à la mode rules.

"Okay, Oliver," I begin. "It's just you and me in here."

"Can we keep the door open?" he asks.

"Why?"

"Because it's a little spooky in here." I look at him and smile because by now I know all of his stalling tactics.

"I just put a new bulb in. It's brighter inside this closet than it is living on the sun. Now let's get started."

"But what if the bogeyman's in here?" Oh, this kid is good.

"He's not," I lower my voice. "He's under your bed, not in my closet!" Oliver's face turns whiter than the vanilla ice cream we're supposed to be having with our pie.

"Reeeaaallly?" he gasps.

"No, I'm teasing. Now let's go, Big Man." I've been calling him "Big Man" since he was born.

I hold up the first card. The letter A is written in red. "Now, what letter is this?"

He looks at me like I'm from outer space. "Are you kidding?" he says. "Do you think I'm a dummy or something? That's an A."

"No, I don't think you're a dummy or something. I think you are smart, really smart. So tell me, what sound does it make?"

"What do you mean?"

I quickly run out of the closet. I hear his voice trailing me into the hallway. "Where you going, Daddy? Do you have to drop a deuce?" He's been using that phrase for the past few months. A gift from his crazy Uncle Matt. My wife's brother also taught him how to light firecrackers in February and finish an entire bag of pretzels at the grocery store before reaching the checkout line.

Downstairs in the kitchen I grab an apple off the tray on the counter. Isabella and Andi are working on a clay project together, and before they can say anything, I'm already back upstairs.

"Did you wash your hands?" Oliver wants to know.

"No, I didn't go poo. I went to get this." I hold up the apple.

"For me?"

"Yes, for you. Now—"

"Can I have a bite?"

"Yes, you can have a bite."

"When?"

"After we do this."

"But why can't I have a bite now?"

"Because I'm trying to do something here. Now please, can we just keep going?"

"Well, you're the one who left."

"Okay, fine. You're right. I did. But now I'm back. Now, what is this?"

"That's an apple . . . An apple you won't let me bite."

"Fine. Take a bite, you little . . . Big Man." He wraps his hands around mine and chomps down like a crocodile. The juice drips down his chin and onto his neck. He wipes it off on my shirt.

"Okay. Now tell me again what this is."

"Apple."

Great. I point to the letter A. "Tell me the sound this letter makes."

"Uhh." I hold up the piece of fruit again with the two-inch forensic impression on it and again I ask him to tell me what it is. Again, he correctly identifies it as an apple.

"Great. Now look at this first letter and tell me what sound it makes."

"Uhh," he says. I wipe my forehead on my shirt. I feel the wetness of the apple juice.

"No, no. Listen. Say it with me." I slowly release the sound of a short "a" from my lips trying to get Oliver to duplicate it.

"'A' like in acrobat or your cousin Adam." And he does duplicate it, perfectly. But when I point back to it on the note card, Oliver repeats "uhh."

"Okay, okay. (Aargh!) Let's come back to A. That's a hard one. How about this?" The letter E is written in shamrock green. "Say it with me." I make the short "e" sound as in elf or end. And he does it, perfectly.

Back to the kitchen. This time Andi asks how it's going.

"Great, great." I say. "We're doing great. We're already on the E."

"Where's the apple?" she asks.

"Uhh, it's upstairs in the closet with Oliver?"

"In the closet. Why is Oliver in the closet?"

"Never mind. It's our man cave. Now where are the eggs?" My entire upper body has disappeared inside the refrigerator as I search for the egg carton.

"Behind the milk." I grab an egg from the container and sprint back up. Two stairs at a time.

Before Oliver can ask, I seethe through my teeth, "No, I did not go poo!"

"Why do you have an egg?"

"Because there weren't any pancakes." He looks at me, confused. "Never mind, I'm kidding. Now, what is this?"

"An egg," he answers. "I just told you."

"Perfect." Then I grab another note card, draw an oval shape on it, and write the word *egg* below it. "What's this look like?"

"An egg."

"Exactly." Oliver points to the note card with the letter A on it now resting next to the bin of Andi's shoes and proudly says, "I'm doing good, right, Dad? I'm getting an A!"

"You're doing great, Big Man." I kiss him on his forehead. His skin is like your favorite pillow. I cover the two Gs in the word *egg*. Pointing to the E, I ask him what sound it makes.

I can see he's taking his time and really trying. He parts his lips . . . "Ohhh."

Over the next few nights, the results are pretty much the same. The vowels are bad enough. The consonants are torture. It isn't his fault. He just has the wrong teacher sitting inside the closet with him.

By the end of the week, I give up. I can't teach this kid—my son—to read. I'm a lawyer, not a magician. So I quit. I quit on my son. There was some small nugget of success, though.

During one of those nights in my *Titanic*-sinking sessions, I noticed the straps on one of my wife's bras sticking out from the top of the laundry bag. "Hey, Oliver," I said, "why do girls wear one of these things?"

He turned a little red and then said, smiling, "To hold their boobies in." Exactly. So I wrote down the capital letter B on a big piece of paper and cut it out with scissors. Then I held it up to my chest and asked him what sound that letter makes.

Without missing a beat, Oliver looked directly into my eyes and made the most perfect B sound you ever heard.

"B, for boobies!" We fell over into each other's arms.

Not long thereafter, I found out just how successful I had been that night. The very next day Miss Vicki, one of the assistant teachers in Oliver's class, called our house. Regardless of the outfit she chooses for the particular day, Miss Vicki is always careful to wear her silver crucifix—and the morals it signifies—for all to see. She informed Andi that during class, when it was Oliver's turn to identify a word, he made the shape of the letter B with his fingers, held them up to his chest, and paraded around the classroom declaring "B is for boobies, Mommy's boobies!"

Small victories.

CHAPTER 3

I'm not alleging that the incident at third base kicked me out of neutral, but Jordan's comments coming out of left field certainly got my attention. They awakened me from my coma, and I suddenly realized my son, a rising fifth grader, was reading at a first-grade level.

There's the saying "Those who can't do, teach." I soon amended that saying to "Those who can't teach, learn." I decided that before I could help teach reading to someone I love, I needed to learn how to teach reading to someone I didn't. Someone who wasn't my kid. So I began looking for how to go about doing just that.

Turns out, a lot of agencies provide services for people who want to learn how to read, but not for people who want to learn how to teach people to read. I never thought much about the word *illiterate* before. I never had to. Those people lived a billion miles away from me. But suddenly I can't stop seeing this word bouncing off the pages of the phonebook. It sounds so clinical, so permanent. As I sit on the floor inside my closet, dialing different numbers, I am overtaken by a heavy haze of sadness. I feel bloated with despair thinking about my little boy in twenty years as an adult unable to read and what that could mean for him.

A recorded message breaks through my malaise: "This is Literacy Chicago. No one is here right now to answer your call. Please leave a message." I don't.

Twenty minutes later I call back. I get the same recording, but this time I leave a message. The kind where immediately afterward you want to break into the building and erase it. Nobody calls me back. So I call again and leave another message, this one almost as humiliating. Nobody calls me back. Finally, on my fourth attempt, I get a secretary who wants to know if I'd like to register for a class.

"I read, I can read just fine." Why would she assume I couldn't read? Perhaps because this organization concentrates on helping adult illiterates learn to read! "You see, my son Oliver, he's eleven, can't—"

"Hold, please." She puts me on hold for almost ten minutes. Eventually a new voice comes on the line.

"Hi, this is June Porter. May I help you?"

"Yeah," I reply. "I was just put on hold for like twenty minutes by someone who for some reason assumed I can't read. I can read. In fact, I just read *East of Eden* in like two weeks."

"Okay, well, that's great, sir. Then how can we help you?"

Wonderful, now new voice thinks I'm drunk! It's the middle of a freaking Monday afternoon and she thinks I'm bloody bombed. Get a grip, Rob. I silently compose myself. The next twenty-nine words out of my mouth better hook this woman like a bass or she'll cut me loose for sure.

"Miss Porter, I swear to God I have not had a single shot of tequila today." Nothing. Not a sound. So I continue. "Not that I don't need one, as you probably could tell by now." She laughs. Actually, for a few seconds.

"Okay," she says, "just take a deep breath. Take your time and tell me how we can help you."

I instantly like her. There's something about her laugh. It's the kind that even over the phone seems as if she's standing right next to you with a plateful of cookies. Like a favorite aunt you wish you saw more often. The laugh vibrates and makes me feel better. I have no idea how old she is, she just feels aunt-like. And I love that when she tells me to breathe, I can hear her breathing with me.

I begin. "I want to learn how to teach somebody to read. You see, I have a—"

She politely interjects. "One second, please."

"Oh dear God, you're not going to put me on hold, are you?" I plead.

"Yes, but just for a second, I promise. No tequila while I'm gone."

She keeps her word and quickly returns. "Okay, continue. By the way, hon, what's your name?"

"Rob. Rob Shindler."

"How old are you, Rob, Rob Shindler?"

"I'm forty-five."

"And you can read, right? Oh yes, I remember now. You finished *East of Eden* in just two weeks!"

"Actually, it was eighteen days." We both laugh.

"Okay, so let's have it, Rob, Rob Shindler. Go ahead and give me the long version." She already knew loquacious me.

At her gracious invitation, I spill the whole gallon. "You see, I have this little boy. My son Oliver. He just finished the fourth grade and he's not such a good reader. He's got these learning issues. I tried to help him, but I almost lost my mind. I felt like ripping out my eyelashes."

She gently interrupts me again. "I'm sorry. You felt like ripping out his eyelashes?"

"No, no. Not *his* eyelashes. *Mine*. My eyelashes. Not literally. That would be painful. But not as painful as trying to get him to read." She laughs. I tell her about our time inside the closet and about SpongeBob SquarePants and how I quit on my own kid. I tell her everything.

"Wait, you quit? You say you quit on your son?"

"Yeah, I quit. I gave up on him." I look away as if she's inside the closet staring back at me.

"So if you quit on your son," she continues, "why are you on the telephone talking to me?" I don't answer. "And why did you leave those two crazy messages on our answering machine and hang up the first time? And then waited on hold for almost ten minutes until Marilyn passed you to me? That doesn't sound like quitting to me."

"You heard those messages, huh? And it wasn't just ten minutes on hold. It was like almost an hour." I pause. "I just want to help him, that's all."

"What's your plan, Rob, Rob Shindler?" I can tell she's now officially teasing me with the rhythmic repetitive name routine. And I like it.

"Well, I figure if I can learn how to be patient and learn how to teach reading to someone at your place, then maybe I can learn how to be patient and learn how to teach Oliver. And maybe then everybody gets to keep their eyelashes." I can hear Miss Porter breathing and thinking and chuckling all at the same time. I haven't even met her in person yet, but I have a strong suspicion we are destined to become friends. "So what do you think? Can you help me?"

Finally she speaks. "You want me to help you help your son, right?"

"Yep."

"So why didn't you just say that at the beginning?"

"I guess I'm a little slow," I answer. "But not at reading. I read—"

"I know, I know. You read . . . really fast!"

CHAPTER 4

Her warm smile is like her laugh. It's welcoming and calms my jitters. She has silver hair and light brown eyes. The color of hot chocolate after a batch of mini-marshmallows has bathed inside the cup for a while. She's wearing a sleeveless apricot dress that falls to the floor. The only jewelry she wears is her gold wedding ring, which you can tell hasn't been removed from her finger in decades. She's effortlessly elegant.

There's a framed painting of Martin Luther King Jr. on the wall, and her desk is plastered with pictures—presumably of family—and Post-it notes in a variety of sizes. Each one has something written on it, from top to bottom, covering every inch and corner. Phone numbers, names, addresses. Places to be, appointments to keep. Some barely hanging on by the tips of their sticky edges, but they don't slip off.

"Can I take your coat?" she asks.

"No, I'm fine, thanks." It's colder inside her cubicle than anywhere else in the building.

"So, Rob, Rob Shindler, tell me about Oliver." I can't believe Miss Porter remembers his name. I think I said it only once, six days ago. "He's eleven, is that right? That probably puts him in the fifth grade?" She's psychic.

"Yes, he's about to begin fifth grade at Walter Newberry Academy. That's a Chicago public school," I quickly add. By dishing up this fact, I'm hoping to establish something valuable about my character—and Andi's. Simple, unpretentious folks. The kind of people who choose to send our kids to a public school in the city.

"That's wonderful. My husband and I felt the same way. But we wanted a backyard so we moved out to the suburbs over forty years ago."

I tell Miss Porter all about Oliver. How he's funny and clever and creative; how I think he can be something really special one day. She stops me.

"So he's not something really special today?"

"No, no, he's great," I explain. "But he can't read. He's got to know how to read."

"Why?"

Why? She wants to know why? I look at the nameplate next to her pencil sharpener wondering if perhaps tequila had been a stand-in for coffee with her frosted flakes that morning.

JUNE PORTER

DIRECTOR OF LITERACY CHICAGO

Then I peek outside her door at all the adults, many over forty, walking the halls of this facility. Right about now, I can either travel the path toward political correctness or be nakedly truthful. Uncharacteristically, I choose the latter. "Because I don't want my son walking in your halls when he's forty."

She smiles. Then she reaches across the desk and takes hold of my hand and I feel my fears and I are in a safe place. "Okay, Rob, Rob Shindler, I'll help you help Oliver. And then you'll make sure that someday Oliver helps someone else's son, deal?"

I nod. I like her so much.

As I stand to leave, I notice a coupon from Baskin-Robbins on the cluttered desk. Buy one get one free. And I find myself wondering what her favorite flavor of ice cream is.

This time I reach for her hand and look into her light brown eyes. "Nice meeting you, Aunt June Porter." I've called her that ever since.

CHAPTER 5

To become certified as a licensed adult reading tutor, each volunteer must fulfill two requirements. First, the person must complete a literacy seminar over the course of three weekends. Second, he or she must sit in on and participate in one orientation session. Unlike the alphabet, requirement B comes before requirement A. Every Wednesday afternoon at exactly 3:00 p.m. (not 3:01), people begin piling in to take their places around one of the ten rectangular tables.

Orientation. No matter how many bodies show up, there's always enough room for everyone. Their leader makes sure of it.

The mild-mannered, elegant lady I met a few days prior has now turned into a New York City traffic cop. "Move over, move over. That's right. You don't need all that space. What do you think, this is your living room?"

A meek-looking woman in her early fifties, who's wearing a cast on her hand that's clutching onto a grocery bag for dear life, stands motionless near the copy machine listening to Aunt June Porter bark out her instructions. "You, yes you, over there. Come, move forward. Don't be shy. Take a seat over there." She directs her toward the back row, where a man wearing parachute pants and wrestling shoes lounges, staring out at no one in particular. "That's right, slick. Crunch the knees together. You don't need to give her an engagement ring, just scooch your butt over."

Although small in stature, Sparkplug is abundant in attitude. I appreciate the full gravity of his appearance only when I decode the totality of his tattoo. A figure of a witch wearing fangs is stenciled underneath his cutoff T-shirt. The image covers the left arm, including his shoulder. But instead of bristles, orange flames are shooting out from the bottom of her broomstick. Finally, bold letters inching their way up his neck in sangria red spell out the word *Kil-I-Man-Jaro*. As in the highest mountain in Africa. Yet, without a sound, Sparkplug crams his knees together out of respect for this silver-haired lady's instructions, as though she's his great-grandmother. The purpose behind orientation Wednesdays is to reinforce Discipline. And Respect. And Responsibility. And Restraint. And Self-Motivation. And Attachment. Being linked to a specific place at a specific time. There's no grading scale or diploma. Every one of the adults present—most of whom are in their thirties and forties—read at a first-grade level or below. Some cannot read at all. Many have come voluntarily, while others have been ordered to attend by either a judge or a treatment facility.

June Porter has only one rule. You must show up for three consecutive Wednesdays. Not one. Not two. Three. If for any reason this continuity is broken, you begin all over again. No exceptions. No excuses. "Those are for the past," in her book. If you're late, you're not allowed in. If you're under the influence, you're sent home. The theory behind Miss Porter's one rule is simple. Most of the people who attend Literacy Chicago's orientation were never able to commit to the educational process. Or the educational process wasn't able to commit itself to them. Regardless, somewhere along the way their education got derailed. By showing up three Wednesdays in a row, the nonreader is showing his or her desire to get it back on track.

Many have traveled inconceivable distances just to claim a seat inside the cramped room. Some take two trains or two buses to get here. When they were children, they wouldn't walk two blocks to go to school. But today is different.

Today they have Miss June Porter. And her routine is simple. She points at you, you stand. Everybody has a story, and you're required to tell yours. She starts off by asking one question: "Why are you here?"

As Chicago's oldest adult literacy organization, the center's mission is to help students become better parents, more productive employees, and citizens who can start giving back to their communities. But a recurring phrase found up and down their website, literacychicago.org, is "to empower them to say 'Now I belong.'" By insisting that each member stand and be accounted for, Aunt June Porter is forcing each to belong. To become part of something. The reason for acknowledging you can't read is because being illiterate is an illness. And as with any illness that goes untreated, it never gets better. In fact, as the condition continues to worsen, it can begin to affect other family members. For example, if a child sees that his or her parent is unable to read, why should he or she care to learn? Illiteracy can feasibly serve to mentor complacency.

When I first heard that Oliver had a learning disability, I was pissed. Really pissed. At everybody, but mostly God. He's always the easiest to rail against. After all, NFL stars always thank Him after scoring a touchdown. Why shouldn't I be able to blame Him after striking out?

But as I sit in this room listening to these people tell their stories, not a single one points a finger upward. Instead they point at their teachers or their parents or themselves. Mostly themselves. They never knew not caring about learning to read when they were younger would preside over every step they would take as adults. Or, more precisely, wouldn't take.

June introduces Lucinda as the center's most recent graduate. "Lucinda, tell everyone about what a great time we had at the prom last week."

The woman slowly rises. Although Lucinda—who quit school after the seventh grade—recently completed her three consecutive Wednesdays, she chooses to still attend orientation. All the new pledges in the room go blank as they look around, wondering what Miss Porter's talking about. Was there really a dance? I hear someone at my table whisper, "Who's going to pay for my tux?"

Miss Porter continues. "Go ahead, Lucy, tell everybody about your beautiful dress. I swear, I have never before in my life seen a shade of red like that. It looked like the sky right before a big storm. How delicious the punch tasted. And how we danced and danced and danced."

The truth is, there was no beautiful red dress. Or punch. Or dancing. Miss Porter was teasing them, just trying to add a note of levity to a stretch of two and a half hours that would be filled with a heavy dose of reality. It worked. A mischievous female voice from one of the tables in the middle yelled, "Was there some calm after that storm, Lady Lucinda?" For a moment, I was transferred back to my own prom and the hotel room the eight of us rented.

"Rob, Rob Shindler," I hear Aunt June Porter call out. "Stand up and tell all these good folks why you're here." Oh my God, I'm seasick. "Go ahead. Come on, everybody gets a turn. Take yours."

I stand and look at all the eyes looking back at me. "Hi, I'm Rob. Rob, Rob Shindler as Miss June calls me." They don't know what to make of me, just as I don't know what to make of them. Adult strangers measure each other with such precise misconception. "I'm here because of my little boy Oliver. He's eleven and he's having trouble learning to read. He has a learning disability." That's probably the first time I ever confessed that in public. I think it's probably the first time I heard myself say it out loud. Suddenly several people who were barely paying attention are now anxiously waiting for me to continue.

"I hate that phrase. Learning disability. I really do. My son is not disabled. He runs fast and can climb tall buildings in a single bound." I think back to being held hostage in that specialist's office and her giving Oliver that test and him wearing those oversized headphones. I smile inside.

"It's leap tall buildings." What? I hear it again. "Leap. Superman leaped tall buildings in a single bound. Not climbed." The correction comes flying out from the back row like a flame of fire. From Kil-I-Man-Jaro.

"You're right. He did leap them, not climb. Thanks." He nods his head at me and then continues filing his nails on the corner of the table.

I explain that I want to help Oliver learn to read, but I don't know how. That I believe if I can learn to help them read, then I can help him. They like my story. The ones who had no fathers come up to me after class and say they wish they had had someone who wanted to help them when they were eleven. Many of them had their own learning disability. Others told stories about their parents beating them or calling them horrendous names just because they couldn't read. How their parents gave up on them.

Some people ask what kind of learning disability Oliver has, and before I can get a word out, all at once they sing out their own respective identifications: ADD, ADHD, dyslexia. One woman is visually impaired. A middle-aged man wearing a cowboy hat is hard of hearing. Most don't know their specific diagnosis, just that they have forever had difficulty learning. I explain that Oliver's issues can't be labeled simply by creating an acronym with three or four consecutive letters.

He's wired differently. Because of his short-term recall, processing, and comprehension deficits, you could ask him what three times five is and he would know the answer. But fifteen seconds later, the answer fades away. Regardless of the difference in their differences, even without meeting my son, the strangers in this room immediately connect and empathize with Oliver.

At the end of their third consecutive Wednesday, attendees finally receive the reward they came for. A tutor. A person who will have the patience, the spirit, and the know-how to guide them to a place where they've never been before. Literacy Chicago is a nonprofit organization that survives because of their volunteer tutors. People from various walks of life coming here for a purpose: to help illiterate adults learn to read. Some volunteers are retired insurance salesmen. Some are recent widows looking for a way to keep busy. And some simply want to help the little boy sleeping in the room down the hall. In the end, individual motivations are irrelevant because hope loves company.

CHAPTER 6

You canNot get into Heaven if you are a homosexual. Homosexuals canNot get into Heaven.

You canNot get into Heaven if you are a weed smoker. Weed smokers canNot get into Heaven.

You canNot get into Heaven if you are a fornicator. Fornicators canNot get into Heaven.

Street Preacher is the first person I see as I approach the building that houses the literacy center where I am about to begin the first day of the collective six-day tutoring seminar. He stands on the corner of Washington and State streets wearing his black suit and brown shoes, working the microphone with his left hand and passing out pamphlets with his right. Pamphlets filled with propaganda about homosexuals, weed smokers, fornicators, and any other heathens who will not be welcomed at the doorsteps of his pearly gates. According to people in the neighborhood, Street Preacher holds court from dawn 'til dusk, delivering his message to everyone who passes by. At the rate he's going, heaven is going to be one lonely destination.

Being downtown on a Saturday morning feels so different from being here during the regular workweek. For instance, I never before paid attention to that drummer sitting on the milk crate playing those plastic buckets. On a busy afternoon at two thirty, with people dashing in every direction, you can't hear him. But today I can. And he's good. No, he's great. He should be playing in a concert hall, not at some intersection. Even the sidewalk under my feet feels different because today I'm wearing my favorite sneakers instead of my fancy lawyer loafers.

I take the elevator up to the ninth floor. Aunt June Porter promised me if I completed the thirty-six-hour seminar, I'd become a certified tutor and, more important, I'd know how to teach people to read. The truth is, I don't care about people. I care about "my Big Man" sitting at home in his PJs watching cartoons. I'm hypermotivated when I enter the classroom.

For the first few hours of the morning session, lecturers—people who either have written books on education and phonics or are experienced tutors—speak to the class and share some of the tricks of their trade. Although each tutor has a different style of teaching, the one characteristic common to all is their extreme patience. Many adults who can't read have had the hope of learning beaten out of them. Literally. When asked why they quit trying, almost every one of them says it was because their teachers had no patience with them. A simple act of rolling your eyes or exhaling in frustration tells a student volumes about your true feelings. If the person trying to help students doesn't believe they can do it, neither will the students themselves.

After lunch, we start from the beginning. Vowels. Short a's and long a's. Long e's and short e's. Short i's, long i's—o's and u's. Consonants. Consonant Clusters. Consonant Blends. When c's sound like c's, but sometimes sound like s's. G's being g's, except when they're j's. The Dolch list* and Sight Words. Word Patterns and Duet Reading and Spelling Strategies. No wonder learning to read as an adult can be so dreadfully painful.

On Sunday we spend a majority of the morning discussing the importance of phonics. Phonics is "the study of the relationship between speech sounds and the letters that represent them." Phonics is sometimes called "decoding" because it's the sounding out of letters in unknown words. Although phonics is not a foolproof system for learning to read, it is a great starting point. By mastering every single possible sound any letter in the alphabet can make at any given time, you can break apart a word from beginning to end until you can figure it out.

We discuss a variety of different learning styles and how it's so important to determine which works best for a particular

* The Dolch list is a compilation of sight words published by education professor Edward William Dolch in 1948. A sight word is a word that you should recognize instantly. Once you see it, you just know it. Specifically, the Dolch list consists of 220 frequently used words found in the classics for children. Dolch believed that after a child (or an adult) had a command of the words on this list, he or she could begin to read successfully.

person. Some people, for example, are visual learners, which means they learn better when they see something, while others are auditory learners, who learn best by hearing. Many teachers teach the way they themselves first learned. Ultimately this can lead to failure because it doesn't factor in what works best for the student. In other words, just because I learned how to read by looking at pictures and writings on the blackboard as a second grader at Shelley Nathanson Grammar School doesn't mean it'll work for Oliver today. "Curiosity may have killed the cat, but creativity can teach someone how to read the word cat," offers one of the lecturers. "Find what works, no matter how unorthodox, and use it to become a valuable tutor!"

The last speaker of the day is Charles, a sixty-three-year-old traveling salesman. Although as well dressed as (if not better than) any of the previous lecturers, and equally eloquent, Charles is neither an author nor an educator; nor is he a tutor. Rather, Charles is a student. He's a handsome, dark-skinned man wearing a perfectly pressed three-piece suit that looks like he was born in it. A classy antique watch hangs by a chain from the pocket of his vest. A pair of bifocals rests effortlessly on the bridge of his nose. He's impeccably groomed. The tops of his burgundy shoes are spotless, as if they just came out of the box.

Charles has just returned from a business trip in Denver. He sells discounted men's clothing in minority sections of major cities around the country. He's been doing this for the past three years. After sharing a few war stories, he explains how he got sick and tired of eating nothing but hot dogs and hamburgers. At first, I thought perhaps he was just a junk food junkie. But that wasn't it. You see, the diners in the motels and lodges he stayed at didn't serve chicken. And since hot dogs and hamburgers and chicken were the only words he could read on a menu, that's all Charles ever ordered. Hot dogs. Hamburgers. And chicken. He was too embarrassed to point to anything else on the menu.

Come again? Certainly this successful salesman can't be illiterate! But he is. And nobody except his family and a few of his closest friends knows it. And now us, of course. Twenty-two perfect strangers endeavoring to become tutors. I don't feel bad for Charles, though. I feel sad for him. How hard that secret must be to keep. Every single day of his life, wherever he walks in those perfectly shined burgundy shoes. And how many different condiments must he find to put on his hot dogs and hamburgers to make them taste a little more palatable each time.

Charles wanted more choices. So he, too, found Aunt June. He's now been studying with a tutor at Literacy Chicago for nearly a year and has dramatically improved. His ability has far surpassed a few words on a diner menu. According to June, it can take a forty-year-old illiterate person four or more years to learn to read with agility. Charles has a long way to go. We all do!

The next weekend, Aunt June Porter marches in a group of eight students to tell their stories. Many, like Charles, have become fixtures at the literacy center. What's amazing to me as I listen to these testimonials, similar to those I heard during orientation Wednesdays, is that nearly every story is the same. Learning to read simply passed these good folks by. And now they live out their days fighting not to be discovered. They memorize bus routes and train schedules and words on a menu so they don't ever have to ask anybody any questions that would reveal what's beneath their disguise.

If Charles's story didn't seal the deal for every volunteer in the room, then Katie's certainly did. Katie is a thirty-one-year-old white single parent who works part-time in a medical supply factory. In between thanking us for being there that day, she explains she can't help her second-grade daughter with her homework. No tears. No bitching. No alibis. Yet she can't camouflage the pain oozing from her as she speaks.

As illogical and incredible as it may sound, I felt like I learned more in those thirty-six hours than I had during six semesters of law school. And at the end of the third weekend, when I received my certificate officially recognizing me as a bona fide Adult Literacy Reading Tutor, I was as proud as I had been after passing the bar exam. While strutting down State Street at 4:30 that Sunday afternoon, I pass Street Preacher again, who is still forewarning people about his top one hundred pastimes that shall keep them out of heaven. Before I know it, I'm sprinting past stoplights, hopping over curbs, and creating sparks on the sidewalk. I can barely wait to get home to see Oliver. Because whether we're sitting in a tiny closet or at the kitchen table or inside the freaking lions' cage at the zoo, I'm going to help him learn to read. Or die trying.

CHAPTER 7

So now that it's official—I have my certificate and my little Literacy Chicago lapel pin to prove it—let me introduce you to my class.

You met UPS Melvin in the first chapter, remember? A few seconds after he and I shake hands and he sits back down, two women walk into the classroom together. I can tell they just met by the distance they are standing from each other. And they're both staring straight ahead like racehorses. I'm not sure which one of the four of us is more nervous. Four deer stranded together waiting to see who moves out of the way first.

"Welcome, come on in," I say. "This nice man is Melvin." As a perfectly dignified gentleman would do at a dinner party, Melvin pushes himself out of a chair two sizes too small for his frame, stands up, and presents his giant hand to each of the two strangers. He doesn't say a word, but his smile seems to thaw the tension of the room, and both women begin talking at the same time.

"No, no, no, you go first," insists the one closest to my desk.

"Okay, well, um, my name is Anne, Anne Marie. It's a real pleasure meetin' you all." Anne Marie is an ice block of a woman. She may not be as tall as Melvin, but she's certainly capable of giving him a run for his money in an arm wrestling match. In one hand she's carrying a Big Gulp cup from 7-Eleven, and in the other there's a family-size bag of Cool Ranch–flavored Doritos. I'm not sure if she's here for a picnic or for our first reading session. She's wearing a powder-blue knitted winter hat that sits high above where the top of her head ends. She looks like Marge Simpson.

"Hi, Anne, Anne Marie. I'm Rob." I remember her from the orientation class a few weeks before because she was wearing the same blue hat. (I would later learn she never goes anywhere without it.) I immediately recognize a similarity between her and Melvin. Oh my God, what a smile. That's two great smiles in less than ten minutes—a record in today's society. There must be three hundred teeth residing inside her mouth, and you can see every last one of them when she smiles! They're flawless and look like she has them professionally whitened. But she doesn't. My parents took out a loan during the course of maintaining their children's dental hygiene, yet our choppers don't come close to Anne Marie's.

As for her counterpart, Elvira is almost the exact physical opposite. She's short, barely five feet tall, and can't possibly weigh more than ninety pounds. Elvira is wearing white gym shoes with blue laces and no socks. She also—chillingly—is wearing traits of both my paternal grandparents on her face. Like my Grandpa Morris at eighty-nine, when he was lying peacefully in his casket, Elvira has skin that is smooth and nearly wrinkle free. I guess she is probably in her late forties. Later, I am surprised to find my guess is off by more than a decade.

I can also see the same soulful eyes I remember my Grandma Sarah having. Elvira is wearing silver-rimmed circular glasses that have been self-repaired multiple times. She constantly takes them off to clean the scratched lenses with the single piece of Kleenex she keeps inside her backpack. As Elvira comes closer, I notice the family of dark freckles—various shapes and sizes—on her face. She reminds me of the actor Morgan Freeman. It will be several sessions before I see Elvira's teeth and her own smile, equal in beauty to Melvin's and Anne Marie's.

On the final day of our tutoring seminar, a seasoned educator had come in to lecture us on the characteristics of adult illiterates and the do's and don'ts of helping them learn to read. He emphasized the differences between teaching adults and teaching children. As tutors, he stressed, we must remember that even though the Elviras and Melvins of the world may read like six-year-olds, their interests, their needs, and their experiences are those of an adult. The way we interact with them must reflect that. They no longer see life through rose-colored glasses and aren't looking for Cinderella endings. They're realistic about their goals and their futures. They no longer want to be president or a CEO of a Fortune 500 company. They now dream these things for their grandchildren. Instead, they simply want to be able to enjoy the sports section in their daily newspaper. Read a menu. Fill out a job application. Understand the instructions on medicine bottles. Help their sons and daughters with their homework. Read the Bible in church. Achieve the self-respect we all take for granted.

The purpose of the first meeting is simply to introduce ourselves to one another. Basically, it's a meet and greet between tutor and students. I start out by asking each of them questions about their lives, but all they want to hear about is mine. What do I do for my job? How old am I? Am I married? How many kids do I have? How far away do I live? Why would anyone want to work for free? "Especially for a stranger," adds Anne Marie. After a few attempts at trying to redirect the conversation back to the three of them, I suddenly get up from my chair, grab my coat, and walk out. I can feel the silence and their confusion behind me. I stand outside with my forehead pressed against the cold wood of the door.

I have no idea why I have walked out. I just did it. Perhaps I need some air. Maybe I am deciding whether or not to just abort the whole mission. Even though I am supposed to be some kind of teacher, I feel like a scared kid. The fact that they are strangers is bad enough. The fact that they are strangers waiting for me to make some change in their life is borderline paralyzing. In the seminar sessions, I kept hearing stories about how these nonreading adults had been let down—in school, at work, at home, in life. Although they are unmistakably sick and tired of being defeated, I can see the sliver of hope in each of them. That is the reason for all of their questions. Not regarding their potential, but mine.

I, likewise, am filled with hope. Not for them, but for the reason I have come to this building in the first place. My son. My motivation is simple and my selfishness—if you want to call it that—has been made clear from the very beginning. So a few seconds later I knock on the door, hear Melvin say, "Come in," and reenter the room pretending our initial meeting a few minutes prior had been a mirage.

"Hi. My name is Robert, but you can all call me Rob." I put my coat over the back of the chair and sit down. They are watching me carefully, analyzing my next move. "Is anyone nervous?" I ask. Nobody raises a hand. I raise mine. "Well, that's good. I'm glad to hear you're not nervous. Being relaxed is a good thing." I look at Anne Marie, who's slurping from the straw in her Big Gulp, but I can still see the corners of her grin curving up behind the full moon of her cup. "I, on the other hand, wore three pairs of underwear here today because I'm scared out of my freaking mind that I may ruin my pants."

They all laugh. Melvin the hardest; Anne Marie the loudest.

"I think everybody needs to know something right from the very beginning before we start. I've never done this before. It's my first time being a tutor, and the truth is, I may stink at it. So just in case I do, I want to apologize to all of you in advance for wasting your time. I wasn't ordered by some judge to be here, and I'm not looking to make sure I get a nice spot in heaven with a window. I'm also not being paid anything to be here. I am a nice person, but not nearly nice enough to come here just because I'm a nice person. I'm busy. I'm a lawyer and I'm married and I have three kids. And I have this little boy at home who is having a tough time at school."

Elvira stops cleaning her lenses and listens intently, holding her face in the palms of her hands. "What's his name?" she wants to know.

"His name is Oliver and he has a learning disability. He can't read. I've tried everything. I even offered to give him my car." Again there's laughter. What they don't know is that this is true!

"What about your other kids, how they all doing?" asks Melvin.

"Well, I have another little boy, Sage, who's seven and is smarter than his father. And Oliver has a twin sister, Isabella, who is doing unbelievably well in school and is a great, great kid. She—"

"Wait a minute," Anne Marie stops me. "You got twins? Oh, man. I always wanted to have twins. That's got to be a hoot."

"So you like being a dad?" Elvira asks, appearing to already know the answer.

"I love being a dad. In the beginning, I'd lie in bed at night hoping to hear a noise, any noise, coming from their cribs just to justify touching them one more time. Seeing their little eyelids opening and adjusting to the dark was like watching them being born all over again."

The two women gaze at me the way females look at a man who's shopping for his wife on Valentine's Day.

"Don't think I'm all that. I'm not," I assure them. "It was way easier when they were babies."

For the rest of the class, we speak about Oliver. They want to know everything. What he looks like. What his hobbies are. What he wants to be when he grows up. They're consumed with the boy who brought them their tutor. When our time is up, we stand, shake hands, and walk out together. We all ride down in the same elevator I had traveled up in with UPS Melvin the Giant just a few short hours earlier. As we exit the building, I share the revolving door with Elvira. She stands in front of me, and as I help push on the glass to make it move, it becomes more evident than ever just how small she really is. An aging woman in a little girl's body. Suddenly, before we are ready to step out onto the city street, she turns her head back and looks up at me through the scratches of her circular lenses. For a brief moment, I swear I think I am with Grandma Sarah.

CHAPTER 8

Three years ago, our family traveled to Africa. Isabella and Oliver were eight; Sage had just turned four.

Before we left Chicago, we purchased each of them a camera from Walgreens so they could capture their own moments during the safari. Andi and I also brought along our high-powered Nikons with which to formally record the trip. The funny thing is, all of our pictures are of Isabella, Oliver, and Sage taking their pictures. We got to see Africa through their eyes.

Every person we knew thought we were crazy and voiced it loudly in chapter and verse. How could we be so reckless as to place three small children's well-being in such obvious danger? *Africa*, of all places? Yet it was the single greatest experience of my life and, I believe, one of the greatest decisions I have made as a parent. Giving our kids the chance to see a scope of reality only inches from their still impressionable and forming characters is something Andi and I will never regret. They saw men and women walking six miles to jobs where they earned a dollar seventy-five. Per day! They visited a Masai village in Tanzania where we were welcomed with open arms into the tribal leader's home constructed of mud, cow manure, twigs, and straw. The Three Little Pigs had nothing on these folks architecturally.

One of the greatest events we witnessed together was watching a herd of elephants cross right in front of our jeep. There were more than thirty of them. Moms and dads with their babies, aunts and uncles, nieces and nephews and cousins. It didn't take long to recognize which ones were the parents. Their maternal and paternal demeanors were immediately evident as they marched past us. They protected what was theirs with ferocious intensity, and although never aggressive, they subtly let us know they were aware of our presence.

Here's the coolest part. They moved as *one*. For instance, with his trunk, the twelfth elephant in line held onto the tail of the eleventh elephant in front of him, who used his own trunk to hang onto the tail of the tenth, who used her trunk to hang onto number nine's . . . and so on . . . and so on. It was an amazing display of unity and grace. And so when Uncle Louie wanted to scratch his belly or Baby Joey needed a breather, they all stopped. They began and ended in concert. No one elephant's itinerary was more important than the next's. It was fascinating to watch. It took almost twenty minutes for them to cross that watering hole, but they all made it, safe and sound.

This was how I decided to move forward as a tutor with my three students. As one. Like that family of African elephants, we would start and stop together. The recurring complaint I heard both in my training and during the orientations I sat in on was how fast school went by in the illiterate adults' earlier lives. A teacher would write ten words on the blackboard to memorize. The following week, there would be another ten. The third week, another ten. Before they knew it, there were fifty new words. If you weren't able to keep up, you became lost. And soon, forgotten. In Africa, if the other members of the family had just kept going when Baby Joey stopped to take that breather, he would have been trampled on or left behind. Soon he would be lost and alone and eventually attacked and killed by a predator—the same as what happens with illiteracy.

As I explain my "Elephant Theory," the look on the faces of Melvin, Anne Marie, and Elvira reminds me of the expressions on my own children's faces as they gazed at giraffes and zebras and lions in Africa. Disbelief and wonder. I promise each of my students we will never move forward without every person feeling comfortable and ready to do so. We will hang onto the tail of the person in front of us and always travel together. I have one final question before we start. "What kind of steps does a baby take?" I ask.

Anne Marie raises her hand. "Go ahead, Anne Marie, tell us," I say.

With a mammoth grin she shouts out, "Baby steps!" I couldn't have rehearsed it better.

"Exactly!" I shout back. "And that's how we're going to learn to read. Taking baby steps."

CHAPTER 9

Phonics is a little like being a detective trying to solve a case. Taking apart an entire word piece by piece and then putting it back together to create a whole word. Perhaps if I had dressed Oliver in a trench coat like Columbo and we went on an excursion in my closet trying to unravel that unsolved crime, we would have been more successful. But that was then and this is now. And for now, I'm going to turn the three people sitting in front of me into junior supersleuths.

Our classroom is equipped with a whiteboard and a blackboard, each hanging from a wall. I write down each vowel in thick red magic marker on the whiteboard. A – E – I – O – U. I explain that these five letters are our gasoline. Without them, we cannot move. There can never be a word for us to read unless it has at least one vowel inside it.

"How many fingers do we have on our hands?" I ask.

"Ten," they yell in unison.

For now, that's the exact number of sounds I need them to memorize. The five vowels and the two basic sounds each one makes. It may sound simple, but it didn't hit me until earlier in that week while I reviewed the phonics section in my tutoring manual. Reading is really made up of just two things: memorizing and sounding out. That's it. If you think about the thousands and thousands of words you know, all you've truly done over the years of reading is commit these words to memory. Whether it's a two-letter word such as "of" or a twenty-five-dollar word like "antidisestablishmentarian," if you know it when you see it, it's because you've memorized it.

Underneath thc letters A, E, I, O, and U on the whiteboard, I write my students' names in black capital letters. MELVIN. ANNE MARIE. ELVIRA. I walk to the other side of the room and switch off the lights. I return to the whiteboard, and after I've erased each and every vowel, I switch on the lights again. What's left are the letters MLVN, NNMR, and LVR. I ask each person to stand, and as if it's teatime at the Four Seasons, I introduce everybody.

"LVR [sounds like Liver], it's my pleasure to have you make the acquaintance of Madam NNMR [sounds like Nmur]. Madam NNMR, may I present MLVN [sounds like Millvn]." The point of the exercise is to demonstrate the importance of a vowel. Without one, the very names their parents honored them with, the only true possessions they own, are changed right before their eyes. Vowels make words. Without them we have, well, we have liver.

And nobody likes liver!

"Let's pretend there's a giant diamond worth a million dollars on the other side of that door," I propose. "Now, don't let sweet Anne Marie's easygoing personality fool any of you. She's a monster when it comes to jewels." Anne Marie pulls down her knit hat over her eyes, bashfully admiring the tiles on the floor. Taking her left hand and holding it in the air, I say, "Madam Anne is going to do anything, whatever is necessary, no matter who she has to tromp on, to make sure that diamond finds a home on this here little pinky!" I notice the nail polish on each finger has been half chipped off. "I mean anything, including knocking big ol' Melvin on his butt."

Melvin holds up his hands, which he's formed into fists, and jokingly jabs them in Anne Marie's direction as if he's shadow boxing. "Now, as Melvin tries to shake Anne off his back, Elvira moves into action like a sly, spotted leopard. She sprints past them, leaps over the table, and heads right for that big ol' diamond."

Although I still can't coax an actual smile out of her, you can tell she's amused by the thought of Melvin and Anne Marie tussling together as she dashes toward the girl's best friend.

"My point is this," I explain. "That diamond is like a word you can't read yet. It may be over there behind some door out of sight, but it's within your reach. It doesn't matter how you get to it. Whether you run, jump, skip, or ride on Melvin's back, it doesn't matter. It doesn't matter whether you memorize it or sound it out, all that matters is that you get there."

Over the course of my tutoring, I developed a lot of silly sayings, symbolic analogies, and corny stories (the cornier the better, as you'll see in the next chapter) to help get my points across. Because even though we traditionally meet only once a week for a hundred and fifty minutes or so, we start in fifth gear and stay there until Aunt June kicks us out.

I credit Benjamin with that advice. An English teacher in Boston for more than thirty years, Benjamin spent two hours during our closing seminar session explaining his strategies behind teaching adults to read. One of the key points he kept reiterating was how adults attend voluntarily. Unlike children, therefore, they can leave whenever they choose. If they're not interested in what you're saying, they will simply stop coming. In addition, unlike kids, adults have jobs. Therefore, when they arrive in the evening for their tutoring sessions, many times they're exhausted. The last thing they want to be is bored to death. Keep them entertained and they will stay awake.

CHAPTER 10

"I have a question," Melvin says, raising his hand. When you first meet Melvin, before he even utters a syllable, you're prepared to be serenaded by Barry White. Instead, you get Mary White. He speaks softly and precisely and at times is barely audible. He is truly a gentle giant. "Why can I never hang onto it?"

"What do you mean?" I ask.

"A word. I can't hang onto it. I mean, I can learn it today, but when I see it tomorrow, it's like I never saw it yesterday. It's gone. Does that make any sense?"

"Melvin, think about this. If you rent your home, at the end of the month your nice landlord can come over and say, 'Hey, Melvin, how's it going? Did you catch the big game last night? I just love what you've done to the place . . . Now, pack up your stuff and be out by morning.'" Melvin and the ladies are nodding. I continue. "But if you own your place and it's truly yours, who can take it away from you?"

"Nobody," he faintly replies.

"Elvira, did you hear Melvin?"

"Nope."

"Melvin, I want that damn landlord to hear you. Now again, if you own your place, who can take it away from you?"

"NO-BODY," he screams. As he does, I suddenly feel very scared for any landlord or anyone else who ever opts to wake the sleeping giant.

"Exactly, Melvin. Because you own it. It's yours and nobody can take it from you."

Elvira interrupts. "What about the bank?"

"Hey, Elvira, Economics 101 is down the hall and to the left," I tease, shooting her a grin. "My point is, it's the same with a word. If you only rent it—if you only see it today, read it once, then forget about it until tomorrow—you don't own it; it's not yours. But if you say it to yourself 157 times and bury it inside your head, it's yours and you'll own it."

I'm not sure if anybody else in the room notices, but when I say the word *damn*, Anne Marie clamps down on her Bible, another accessory she carries to class in addition to her stash from 7-Eleven. Her Bible. A quick glance reveals it is old: Scotch Tape holds the front cover together, along with sections of pages blotted with varying degrees of yellow and brown from coffee and soda stains.

I later find out Anne Marie's mom gave it to her daughter just before she passed away.

The way Anne Marie grips that Bible gives me an idea.

Another thing Benjamin from Boston encouraged us to do was to tailor the lesson plans and the ways we interact with our adult students to reflect their lives. A child may not relate to a story from the Bible, but the three adults sitting in front of me might.

"Remember the ten sounds I've asked you to memorize? The first five are easy. The vowels are A, E, I, O, and U. They are just simply their names. So Elvira, Mr. A walks into the restaurant and introduces himself by saying, 'Hey everybody, I'm A.' And Melvin, when Miss E follows in right after him, she says, 'Hello, everyone, I'm E.' Now Anne Marie, later that week when Ms. I is late for church on Sunday because she overslept, after services she politely walks up to Pastor Jones and, like any good Christian, holds out her hand and says, 'Mornin' Pastor Jones, I'm Miss I, and I'm awful sorry I was late today.' And then Pastor Jones introduces her to the congregation's newest members, Mr. O and Mrs. U. And that's five of the ten sounds we need to know.

"By the way, speaking of church and Pastor Jones reminds me of a story about a famous couple from the Bible. Now you all know what a beautiful woman Eve was. But did you also happen to know Eve was a very vengeful girl? She didn't exactly like Adam always wanting to watch his precious football all those Sunday afternoons. You see, Adam was a huge New Orleans Saints fan." Melvin is amused, but Elvira and Anne Marie seem a bit confused. "So one day to get back at him, just for spite, she gave him what?"

The three answer in unison: an apple.

"Right! And the second sound for our first vowel is a short one, 'a' for Apple.

"Another little secret you may not know about beautiful Eve is she was one awful cook. I mean, rotten. Let's just say the sales sticker was still inside the oven."

Anne Marie grabs onto that Bible of hers. "How rotten was she, Anne Marie? Eve was so rotten she couldn't boil water. And even when she was lucky enough to get it bubbling, she burned what at breakfast?"

This time the unison answer, eggs, is accompanied by a few chuckles.

"So the second sound of our second vowel is 'e' for Eggs. Now I know after hearing this, you all are too smart to ever sit down at the breakfast table to eat any of Eve's cooking. But if you were brave enough to ever try it, after tasting those burnt, crusty eggs, you would say what, Melvin?"

After a few tries, Melvin lands on the answer: Ick.

"Those eggs are Icky. The second sound of our third vowel is 'i' for Icky."

Only two more to go.

"After Melvin passes out from eating those icky, burnt, overcooked, crusty eggs, we all carry the sleeping giant on the bus together and get him to the nearest hospital as fast as humanly possible. When the doctor finally comes in the room holding one of those dreadful, oversized wooden Popsicle sticks we all remember hating so much, he tells Melvin to open his mouth and say what?"

ANSWER: Ohhhhh.

"The second sound of our fourth vowel is 'o' for Ohhhhh.

"By the way, we remember to bring a sample of Eve's eggs with us so they can be tested by Poison Control. Accidently, while walking in the front door to the hospital, we drop a couple on the ground. A poor, naive bird comes flying by, thinking today's his lucky day. Lunch! So he swoops down and scoops up the eggs with his tiny feathered wing. Later as we come walking out of the building with our saved friend, guess who's flying right above our heads? Let's just say we better not look where?"

Now even Elvira cracks a smile as Melvin answers for them: Up.

"The second sound of our final vowel is 'u' for Up.

"The moral of the story: Never look Up after an angry bird just tasted some of vengeful Eve's Icky Eggs. Instead, open your mouth, say Ohhhhh, and have an Apple!"

CHAPTER 11

As I walk to the lot after my first actual class, I wonder if my Adam and Eve story has just violated every word of another sage piece of advice Benjamin had given us: "Adults are used to being treated as mature persons. Remember, many of them are parents and even grandparents. Do not talk down to them." These are three adults. Elvira is sixty-three and the mother of a Chicago police officer. Anne Marie is forty-two, a housekeeper at the ritzy Congress Hotel who helps her aging father run their home and care for her teenage cousin, who lives with them. Melvin is in his late thirties and employed at UPS as a mechanics apprentice. His job site is an hour and a half from the literacy center. Did he really take two trains and a bus just to hear my silly story about Eve and her lousy cooking?

Yet the following Wednesday evening, there they are. Each has arrived for class at least fifteen minutes before me. Elvira arrives almost an hour early. They are all sitting in their chairs and have their pencils and pads of paper ready to rock 'n' roll. So that's just what we do. After a few pleasantries, we dive in. I write the vowels on the whiteboard. A, E, I, O, and U. I will repeat the entire Adam and Eve story each week, verbatim, reviewing the two respective sounds every vowel makes. This becomes our Pledge of Allegiance. It's how we start every class. And the story always ends the same way: "When an angry bird with indigestion flies over your head, never look Up!"

Then I write every other letter in the alphabet from B through Z up on the board. The consonants.

"The only difference between us and a kindergartner is the boy or girl usually learns how to read the word first and then identifies some object with it later. Adults learning to read do it backward. In other words, we know what a fan is because we're the people who have to buy one in the middle of July to make sure our kids are nice and cool. We don't know how to read the word yet, that's all.

"Or computer. Or Light switch. Or desk. We know what all these things look like because of experiences in our lives. We've seen a computer or flipped off a light switch. Because the kindergartner may not have to pay the electric bill, right, Melvin? But we adults do!"

Then I go around the room pointing to every object I can find and ask them to tell me what it is. Chair. Globe. Television. Cabinet. Wall. Table. Book. Shelf. Eraser. Ceiling. Bulb. Telephone. Outlet. Doorknob. Closet. Lock. Paper. Glass.

Flower. Pot. Coffee. Lamp. Machine. Soap. Dispenser. Stapler. Cockroach. Cockroach!

After killing the cockroach with the stapler, I continue. This time I point directly at them, asking each one in turn to identify their own objects. Their answers come in 3-D stereo. Elvira: Glasses. Melvin: Mustache. Anne Marie: Necklace. Melvin: Cross. Anne Marie: Sweater. Elvira: Tissue. We do this for a few moments, but at such rapid-fire speed we easily identify a hundred different possessions. The point of the exercise is to show them that, collectively, they know a million words already. And soon they will be able to read them on a whiteboard or in a newspaper or on a menu.

"Melvin, how did you find this building when you came here a few weeks ago?" I ask.

"Well, the lady who answered the phone gave me directions."

"Kind of like a treasure map, right? Even if she didn't give you the exact address and just gave you a bunch of small clues, you would have been able to get here."

"Okay, I guess," he agrees, nodding his head.

I bang home my point. "She could have said, 'Look for the building with the big clock on its side, take a right turn and walk fifty-six steps until you see the billboard with the camel smoking the cigarette, then make a left until you hear the preacher man yelling into his microphone, go through the revolving doors right next to where he is standing, and take the elevator up to the ninth floor.' Trying to read is like following a map. Every letter has a sound, we put all the letters, sounds, together, follow the map, and we find our treasure."

Corny, but true. I am on a roll. "So we are going to find twenty-six words we all know and love and attach each of these words to a single letter in the alphabet so whenever each of us sees that specific letter, we'll automatically think of that word. We'll think of the first sound that word makes and then we'll know the sound of the letter attached to that word. The more sounds we memorize, the more treasures we'll find."

To someone who already knows how to read, this may seem rather simplified—ridiculous, even. But to someone who hasn't learned yet, it's the first step up the ladder. And you can't take the third step or the fourth step until you take that first one. Think about when you learned how to swim. The freezing water terrified you so much that getting into the pool or lake was at times even harder than learning the actual strokes. Once you felt comfortable enough in the water, you could transfer your attention to what needed to be learned next. Eventually you forgot how cold the water was and started swimming.

It's the same with adults learning to read, except they are so terrified about the process they become paralyzed even before they test the temperature of the water. When they see an eight-letter word, it's equivalent to swimming across the Atlantic Ocean, and they know how impossible a feat that would be. So they drown before they even stick their big toe in. If they can get comfortable with each and every sound, seeing any given letter as its own miniature word, then with time they will join all the sounds together to form the actual word. In other words, they paddle around in the bathtub before conquering the Atlantic.

I switch gears once more and use another analogy. "A word is like a family." I look and point to Melvin. "One letter is like that lonely guy hanging out at a singles bar looking for true love. When he finally finds her and they get married, they're now a couple. A two-letter word. They then start their family and have a baby. Let's call her 'Melvina.'" He smiles. "So they become a three-letter word. A few years later, they're blessed with twins. Welcome to the club! Now they're a family of five. The bigger the family, the bigger the word. But remember, it all started with that one lonely guy hanging out at the bar."

With the time left, we assign a favorite word to each letter on the board. Triggers. Words that will automatically trigger a certain sound in their minds so when they see that letter in a word, rather than worry about the entire word all at once, they will break it up sound by sound by sound by sound. We vote on each word we'll use. To six-year-old Tommy, the letter B may instantly make him think of bat or ball. But to sixty-three-year old Elvira, who grew up helping her mother make homemade cherry pie, the letter B stands for bakery. And although little Veronica may fondly associate the letter C with her favorite kitty cat, Melvin the mechanic, who works in a garage and has permanent oil stains under his fingernails, immediately thinks carburetor. And when Stephanie turns seven her mommy and daddy may surprise her with third-row tickets to see Hannah Montana in concert, but all forty-two-year-old Anne Marie can think of when she sees the letter H is how she wants to someday learn how to read her horoscope.

It works! We work until every letter is accounted for, and from that day forward, whenever any of us sees one of these letters inside class or out, we are automatically reminded of the one word we have assigned to it.

Their favorite sequence of the alphabet is L-M-N-O-P.

The most important word in the dictionary?

"Love."

And who do we love more than anyone?

"Mom."

What word do we never say to mom?

"No."

And how do we live our lives?

"Powerfully."

That night, I can't help but toot my own horn—albeit humbly—to Andi and the kids. I can't lie, I am proud of the progress we are making. And I am falling in L-U-V with Melvin, Anne Marie, and Elvira. Although the stock market has recently taken a dramatic turn for the worse, I am feeling a huge return on my tutoring investment.

INSIDE O'S MIND

A few weeks before Halloween, Oliver and I are sitting at the beach together talking about how school is going. He has just begun fifth grade, and it is one of those rare gifts from the weather gods when a mid-October day miraculously reaches seventy-three degrees. Just warm enough to sit in the sand with your son without wearing any shoes or socks and whip stones into Lake Michigan for one last time until next year.

"Did you see that? Did you see that?" Oliver wants to know. "That one skipped five times!"

"That's amazing, Big Man." It is only three skips, but dads' discretion allows for the "two extra rule" to apply when necessary.

As I look down at his toes dangling off the pier trying to touch the top of the pre-winter arctic water, it is mind-boggling to see Andi's feet and mine in a miniature Xerox copy. Big toe hers, little one mine. As Oliver moves into my lap, I wonder how much longer he'll feel comfortable and at ease with public affection. Will next year be the year he stops holding my hand as we walk down the street?

I ask him about reading. How it's going. Has it gotten any easier?

"I like math more. I'm better at it," he says. How's that even possible? Nobody likes math better! He likes school, even though "it's just getting harder."

"The work?" I ask.

He pauses. "No, just kind of everything," he answers as he looks out at one of the last birds flying high in the autumn sky.

Oliver splits his day between time spent in the special ed classroom and the general classroom with all the "regular" kids—a concept better known as being "pulled out." Think of it this way. You are sitting inside a movie theater with all your friends and suddenly as the clock strikes twelve, the spotlight comes on and singularly you are summoned to stand and leave.

I have no idea why I choose this day to ask him to explain, but suddenly I have this uncontrollable need to know what it is like to be him. So I ask.

"Hey, Big Man, tell me what it's like when it's time for you to leave your one class and go see Miss McLain in your other."

So in his own words, Oliver allows me to walk in his shoes

as he crosses over from one universe into another. One step at a time.

7:47. Phew, I made it. By the skin of my skinny little butt. I really like saying ass much better. It feels so great coming out of my mouth. I like saying the S part at the end for as long as I can hold my breath so I don't have any more air like when I let everything out of a balloon. Asssssssssssssss. When I'm by myself, I can say it as much as I want. Ass. Ass. Ass. Ass, ass, ass, ass, ass! But with the whole quarter in the penalty jar thing it's really dipping into my savings. Okay, there's Ms. Hazer. Right on time. She's always right on time. I think she sleeps in that classroom. Right on her desk. I hope I don't get a tardy. Oh no, I forgot my Social Studies book on the kitchen counter. It's Mom's fault. She only told me fourteen times. I need fifteen. Fif-teen. A multiple of 3 and 5. And 8. No, not 8. 3. And 5.

8:01. Only six hours left until I get to watch TV again. I hope *Jimmy Neutron* taped.

8:47. What's with Abraham Lincoln's beard? Did he truly want to look like that? I wonder if he lost his razor right after he shaved the mustache but before he got to the beard part and then just got too busy with all the president stuff. Or maybe he just forgot.

8:50. And why isn't he on the quarter?

9:13. I sure hope *Jimmy Neutron* taped. I know I pressed the record button. I'm pretty sure I did . . .

9:35. Man, is Emily Beckert pretty. I wish I sat next to her instead of Antonio. She looks like that girl who works at the movie place who always gives us the giant box of popcorn even though she only charges us for a medium. Except Emily is taller. Way taller. Why can't I be taller? I wonder if she would like me if I was taller. Antonio smells like feet.

11:15. Five minutes to go.

11:16. Four minutes.

11:17. Three minutes.

11:18. Two.

11:19. One . . .

11:20. Blast off. Time to blow this Popsicle stand. Uncle Matt always says that before he leaves our house. Now he's got a great beard. And he kept the mustache and beard and everything. I think that's because he has a lot of time because Grammy always says, "That Uncle Matt's got nothing but time on his hands." Time for Miss

McLain's class. Holy cow! This backpack weighs a billion pounds. Shit. I mean, shoot. I dropped my ruler. It gets so quiet every time I get ready to leave. Ms. Hazer stopped talking. I really wanted to hear how Abe got shot. And why did they let that Mr. Booth bring a gun into the play anyways? Don't they have one of those metal detectors like they have at the airport? "Sorry." I did it again. I can't believe I hit Sam again in the head with my backpack. He's got a huge head, that Sam. Just like George Lopez. That reminds me, only eight hours until *The George Lopez Show* comes on. My all-time favorite show. He's got a ginormous head. Not bigger than Sam's, but still pretty ginormous. I love the one where George is a baby but still has the same size head. He's so funny.

Sam can't be only eleven. Not with that head. And he's as tall as Principal Beaudoin. My dad always asks Sam where he parks his car at school. I always laugh after he says it but I'm not sure why. Sam always laughs when it's time for me to leave. And I don't even say anything funny. Sometimes I really hate leaving. Well, I don't hate it. I just don't like it. They say I have trouble focusing. I focus just fine. If I close both my hands and put them together on top of each other and make a telescope with them and squint my eyes just right, I can see all the way across the room. I can focus really good.

11:22. Sam's not laughing anymore. He's rubbing the back of his head. Adios, gordo de cabeza. That means "fat head" in Spanish. I learned it on *Dora the Explorer*. I learn a lot of great stuff from TV. I like it when the hallway is empty like this. It's all mine. One day, I'm gonna be able to touch that ceiling. There's Isabella's locker. Should I hide her coat again? That window is still broken after Johnny DiDenbetto threw a can of Mountain Dew through it. That guy's car is getting a ticket. He's gonna be really pissed. Sorry. Upset. Hey, I'm all alone and this is my hallway. PIIIISSSSSEDDD!

I'm thirsty. We already had our drinking fountain break before. But I can have another. And take as loooong as I want. Nobody's behind me. I could drink the whole thing if I want to. Now that would be funny. Gordo de cabeza comes and presses the button down and . . . nothing. Let's see how he laughs at that! This pencil definitely is not pointy enough. I'll use the library's sharpener. I could be on *Dancing with the Stars*. That move I did last night in the living room was so awesome. I wonder what my class is doing right now. I bet they already got to the shooting part. Does the bullet make a hole in his hat? That's one tall hat. I bet the guy sitting behind him at that play couldn't see the stage so good. Why'd that guy Mr. Booth shoot him anyways? On TV there's always a hundred people around the president when he's walking someplace. You can't even see his head.

11:26. I hope that kid Ari is not in Miss McLain's class today. Those bird noises he makes make me crazy. I don't care if I am a bad focuser. Nobody could concentrate with bird noises going on all over your head. Okay. I better go. They're probably looking for me by now. Man, I'm thirsty. One more drink. And what about Evan asking me like ten thousand catrillion times how many bathrooms we have. "How many bathrooms do you have . . . how many bathrooms do you have . . . how many bathrooms do you have . . ." And no matter how many times I tell him, he keeps asking me the same question. And I'm the one with the focusing problem, huh? He has ADD or AFT or something with three letters. Why didn't they give me any letters for my thing? Oh my God, how am I supposed to learn my multiplication tables with bird noises all over my head and all the questions about how many bathrooms I have? I hope Jose's at my table. He's so awesome. He weighs like five thousand pounds. And he can burp and sing the "Star-Spangled Banner" song all at the same time. I don't know how he does it. The best is when he does it at the drinking fountain in front of the whole class. Water comes shooting out just like a sprinkler. I'll bet they're already done talking about Abe Lincoln. He was really tall. I bet he could touch the ceiling.

CHAPTER 12

It's our sixth class together, and we're ready to begin talking about consonant blends and consonant clusters. The blend is where two consonants are joined together and you hear each separate sound. For example, BR= BRother, FL= FLag, SW= SWim. By contrast, the cluster is where the two consonants come together to make one sound. For example, CH= Church, SH= SHut, TH= This.

As I've previously stated, to the person who already reads, the substance of this material may seem comically simple. But it's not. It's hard work for my three students, and it's taken enormous effort on their part just to learn what sound or sounds each of the twenty-six letters of the alphabet makes. We've spent every second of our time together using our designated words to trigger the specific sounds each letter makes.

If there are five letters in a word and Elvira knows three of their sounds, she'll be able to figure out the word. At least, that's the hope.

I decide to keep riding the same train that got me here. "All right, Melvin. I know you like being a bachelor, but it's time to make an honest woman out of Anne Marie." Anne Marie stops sipping from her Big Gulp and puts the cup down. She looks confused and concerned. I'm not sure Melvin's her type. "Now that we own the sounds of all the letters in the alphabet, we need to start putting them together. Start creating families." Anne Marie is breathing again and has put the straw back between her teeth.

"I told you my wife and I have twins, remember? Oliver's twin sister is Isabella. Now, after they were born, do you think I would deliver Isabella to Elvira and just hand over Oliver to Melvin? Of course not. I mean, I like you both, but I can't just give you my kids. My wife would kill me."

They laugh. Elvira snorts—a glorious snort that I forgot to mention earlier. For the last few weeks, Elvira's been laughing. A lot. Maybe because she didn't have a lot of practice doing so before, she seems to really like it. In fact, unlike most people who smile and then laugh, Elvira does it backward. Her laugh leaps out first and her smile follows a short while thereafter. I think it stays behind waiting to make sure it's safe.

"So, just as I would never split up my twins, we don't split up our class's twins. Our twins are the consonant pairs. And we never separate these consonant pairs."

I go to my trusty whiteboard and write these consonants—blends as well as clusters—in rows:

BL DR PL SK SQ WR

BR FL PH SL ST

CH FR PR SM SW

CL GR SC SN TH

CR GL SH SP TR

Just as we did with single letters of the alphabet, we need to find ways to trigger the sound of each pair of consonants. Rather than using identifiable catchwords to activate their recall ability, though, this time we select catchphrases to spark their memory. We create prompters aimed at allowing them to automatically recognize a sound the moment they see the given two letters together. The spicier or zanier, the better! Here are a few samples:

- BR= Not your sister, but your BRother.
- CH= Sitting in here together is like being in CHurch.
- CL= Before, we used to always stare at the CLock in school. Now, we never do.
- GR= Tony the Tiger says, "It's GReeaattt!"
- PL= The first word people should learn is PLease.
- PR= Everyday everyone should PRay.
- SK= Reading is like SKating.

- SW= SWim, even when the water is cold.

By learning all the sounds, they begin putting them together and slowly start forming words—aka reading.

Although I never officially give homework assignments, they each admit to practicing their letter recognition when they are at home, at work, out shopping, and even in the shower. As good as I have felt about the process, I sense the trio are also singing their own praises. I can see it on their faces and even in the way they sit higher in their chairs. They are making progress, and my heart is beating like a DRum!

CHAPTER 13

The day had finally arrived. I'd been tutoring Anne Marie, Elvira, and Melvin for almost three months. It was time to take on another student. A much more difficult student. A student who didn't drive or hop on the bus or ride two trains to get to class. A student I had been shying away from for an eternity. And even though he weighed less than seventy pounds and couldn't reach the belt buckle around Melvin's waist, I was much more terrified of him than I could ever be of the Jolly Giant. It was time to take on Oliver.

Although the phrase "It takes a village . . ." is universally overused, it could be no more true than was the case for our son. The fact that the teachers, the caseworker, the counselors, the slew of weekly tutors were all trying to help Oliver was beyond imagination. But the mayor of the village was Andi. She was fluent in every detail there was to know about Oliver's particular learning disability. Every night, as I hid out in my office or at the gym seething in my denial, Andi was at home, working with Oliver. She had created dozens and dozens of color-coordinated 3 x 3 note cards with hundreds of one- and two-syllable sight words and others from the Dolch list for him to commit to memory. She was relentless in her pursuit, and because of her he eventually mastered each and every one of them. When he was having difficulty with his dexterity, she was the one who met with the occupational therapist every day after school and eventually taught Oliver how to write. It should be crystal clear: If there's a hero in this story, it's Andi.

Here are just a few of the words that found permanent homes in Andi's legendary land of little white note cards. (For a complete list, you can Google "Dolch list" and find the 220 words on a number of websites.)

about always around
because better big call
clean cold did down
drink eat eight every
fall fast funny go good
grow help her him if
is it jump just keep
kind know laugh like

little made many must
never new now of old
over play please pretty
ran right round saw
say sing take thank
together under up
upon very walk warm
which yellow yes

Oliver recognized hundreds of words because of his mom. Now it was my turn to take the baton and join his team.

CHAPTER 14

I remember my first. You always remember where you were when it happened. It's exhilarating yet traumatic at the same time. There it stands, all alone. One lonely soldier poised at attention. When it was my turn, I couldn't believe it; I'd been waiting for years. But here it was, right where everyone said it would be. It must have arrived while I was asleep. An overnight delivery from the follicle fairy. "My first pubic hair!" I shouted.

And that's exactly how Oliver's screech sounds when he yells for me as I walk toward his room. I thought he'd fallen off the bed or something, but when I enter, he's looking at himself in Andi's portable magnifying mirror with pride. He's lying on his bed with his jeans down over his knees, holding the mirror above his private area and his head bent closely over the mirror. My son the contortionist.

"Dad, Dad, Dad. Come quick. Look at it. Just look at it. Isn't it amazing?" He's pulling on the poor thing like it was the finals in a game of tug of war. "Come here and look at it, now," he orders me again.

The truth is, initially I can't see it. But as I get closer, there it is . . . a single blond strand. My little boy's first sign of becoming not my little boy anymore. It is somewhat depressing, but Oliver's enthusiasm over his new favorite toy is contagious and eventually I join in on the celebration.

"Okay, okay. Let me see it." I say. I have to admit, it is a beauty. "Wow, that thing is awesome. You can climb that sucker."

"Do you want to touch it?"

Do I want to touch it? It's not like it's a guinea pig we just got at the pet store, for God's sake. "No, um, that's okay. Not right now. Maybe later. Just be careful, though. You don't want to pull it out."

"It's pretty unbelievable, right?"

"Unbelievably unbelievable!" I agree.

"Do you think I'll get any more?" he wonders.

"Big Man, I predict you're going to have a forest down there before you know it." He smiles that Oliver smile and bends back to stare into the mirror at the pubes' reflection. How many times do you get to share such a moment with your first son?

We speak about his hair and the ones to follow for the next forty-five minutes or so. He has other questions, which include but are not limited to: (a) Who was the first girl I liked? (b) What is French kissing? (He even makes me demonstrate the process with my tongue using the magnified mirror as my kissing partner!) And (c) What exactly is third base?

"And don't keep telling me it's the position I play in little league," he warns.

But before I share all my wisdom with him, I have my own list of demands. If he wants the key to these locked secrets, he's going to do something for me.

"What?" he wants to know. "I already cleaned up all the Legos in the basement."

"No, you don't have to clean up anything or wash your hair or even brush your teeth. Nothing like that."

"Then what?"

"Read with me."

He turns the exact same color of his new hair. Probably because this is the first time I've suggested this particular father-son activity since the fiasco in the closet. He quickly recovers enough to drive a pretty hard bargain. I think he still laughs to himself about how well he played me that fateful evening. I made out with that mirror so much we're scheduled to go bowling together next Saturday night. But in the end, Oliver agrees. We have a deal. It is now official. We pinky promise and everything. We plan to meet in his room the next evening after dinner for our first session and he will give it the old college try.

"But remember, I'm only in fifth grade," he insists.

The next afternoon, I pick him up after school and we go to the bookstore together. I want him to pick out his very own book. Something he likes.

"Why do I need a book?" he asks.

"Because we need something for you to put your glass of milk on in bed while you're watching TV."

"Really?"

"No. I have an idea, and I want you to read something you like."

"But I don't know how to—"

I stop him. "Just do this for me, will you, Big Man? Pick something."

We walk around the first floor for a while and then finally take the escalator up to the second, where the classics are. And the coffee shop that also sells cookies. After downing a kid's caramel frappuccino and two vanilla scones, he's finally ready to choose something.

A bit of Shindler family history plays in to why Oliver picks the book he does. A few months earlier, Andi and I took Isabella and Oliver to this little ranch in the suburbs where you could fish in a stocked trout farm and ride horses. Over the years, the twins had each ridden small ponies at Halloween festivals and local carnivals, but this was their first time on a real horse, sitting up on a saddle and locking their feet in the stirrups.

Two horses were left in the stable, a black one and a brown one. Both were stunning, but Oliver had his sights on the black one. Unfortunately, so did Isabella, and a big fight ensued over who would ride which horse. A big fight always ensues between twins whenever a choice is involved, especially when one of the twins is Oliver P. Shindler, the Shotgun Kid. He wants to have first choice in everything. Front seats in automobiles, windows on airplanes, places on couches, sticks of chewing gum, etc.,

etc., etc. And he usually gets his way simply because he wears his opponent down. But on that day we let Isabella win, and Oliver proceeded to pout the whole way along the trail as he rode on Rocky, his beautiful brown Italian stallion.

Today we stroll down the aisles in Barnes & Noble. "*Black Beauty*, what a wonderful selection," the cashier says. "I've read it at least ten times myself. You are going to love it. Why did you choose this particular book, young man?" she inquires.

Without missing a beat, Oliver looks her right in the eye and in a somewhat diabolical voice answers, "Because I don't like brown ones!"

When we get back in the car, I feel quite proud. Yesterday his first pubic hair, today his first big boy book. I drop him off at the park behind our house to meet up with some of his friends and I go back to my office downtown to finish up some work. As I drive off, I roll down the window and call out to Oliver, "Meet you in your room after dinner, right?" He doesn't answer. Instead, his walk turns into a jog, which turns into a full-blown gallop. It is as if he is Black Beauty, a racehorse sprinting to the finish line. Or running away from it.

Later on, when I arrive home, I kiss everyone hello and head right for the stairs. On my way up, Andi passes me a turkey sandwich she has made me for supper. The whole family knows I've declared tonight as "This is the day" night. When I walk into Oliver's room, his face—as usual—is glued to the television, so close to the screen that I don't even know how he sees anything.

"Let's do some reading, Big Man," I say.

"Not yet," he sings under his breath, not even blinking.

Sometimes, I swear to God if I hadn't helped make this kid, I'd deck him! Patience, Rob, patience, I grumble under my breath.

"Come on, we had a deal."

"Just one more *Jimmy Neutron* episode, Dad. It's the one where he turns himself into a chipmunk."

"You mean the one where he turns himself into a chipmunk that you've seen 687 times?"

"I have not!" he protests without looking up.

"You have too."

"Have not."

"Have too." My little chipmunk has me running around like a gerbil on a wheel inside my head.

I catch a glimpse of the yellow clown bank sitting on Oliver's dresser. His bulging green eyes are glaring at me. Like the *Mona Lisa*, his gaze follows me around the room wherever I stand. I get more eye contact from this melted piece of plastic than from my own son. The clown is half filled. A shiny silver dollar is stuck in the middle, which makes it look like he has a belly button. "Hey, Oliver. How would you like that cool motorized ATV we saw at Toys 'R' Us last week?"

His head slowly turns away from the television, and my mannequin finally blinks as if he's just come out of a hypnotic trance. "You mean the all-terrain vehicle with the two different speeds and the towing hook attached to the back? With the radio that really works. Are you serious, that one?"

"Well, the radio doesn't really work; it's just there for show," I clarify.

"Does too."

"Does not . . . okay, whatever. We'll get you a radio you can hold onto while you're zooming around the sidewalks of Chicago. Now can we please turn off the TV?"

I pick up the bank. "All right, you see this suction cap on the bottom of Mr. Scary Clown?" He nods his head. "If I took this cap off and shook the clown up and down really hard, what would happen to all the coins inside?"

"They would all fall out. And you'd have to pick them up, not me. Right?" Breathe, Rob, breathe.

I continue, "But if I keep the cap on, no matter how hard I shake that bank, the money will stay in, right?" I have his attention now, even though he's still hanging onto the remote control like it's the antidote to some deadly disease. "Well, it's the same with words. If you learn a word—I mean, really, really, really learn it—then (pointing to his head) it goes inside your bank. And no matter how hard you shake it, the word will stay inside. It will be yours. Forever."

Oliver begins shaking his head from side to side, trying to see if he can actually disconnect it from his neck. "Okay, enough. You're freaking out Mr. Scary Clown." We both look at the bulging green eyes following us around the room.

"So can I really get that cool motorized ATV with the towing thing on the back and the two different speeds with the radio that really wor—"

"Yes, yes." Sometimes I wonder if I'll ever get the hang of this whole dad thing.

"When, when?" he wants to know. "Tomorrow. How about tomorrow? Can I get it tomorrow?" He's in fourth gear and about to move into fifth.

"No, not tomorrow."

"Well, when?" he interrogates me with his arms folded.

"You want to hear my idea or not?"

"Fine!" Unfolding his arms, he falls back on his bed.

For every word he reads in the book we just bought, he gets a penny. For every letter he sounds out correctly in a word he doesn't know, he gets another penny.

"A penny. Are you kidding me? A penny! Mom is right. You are cheap."

I explain that when he finishes the whole book, he should have enough money to buy his new motorized toy.

"This whole book?" he says as he holds it up over his head. "That's like a billion pages!"

"I hope not, because I don't have that many pennies in my bank account."

"Okay, fine," Oliver concedes as he blows air out of his mouth like he's blowing out candles on his birthday cake. "I'll start tomorrow."

"No, you'll start tonight," I respond with sudden authority. He glares at me as if he wants to hit me in the nose with the book. And then he lies back against his pillows and opens up *Black Beauty* to the first page.

"How much do I need to buy that ATV?"

"Well, let's see. It costs 360 dollars."

"How many pennies is that?"

"Um," I pause. I needed a moment to figure it out. In reality, a few moments. "Okay. There's a hundred pennies in a dollar. One thousand pennies in ten dollars. Ten thousand pennies in a hundred dollars. So . . . you'll need thirty-six thousand pennies to get that ATV."

"Whhhhhhhhaaaattt!" he yells. Oliver's face scrunches up and his eyes get all squinty until they disappear. "Thirty-six thousand. That's, like, almost a billion!" (Mathematically speaking, the apple doesn't fall far from the tree.) "I'll never have that much. I have to read, like, the whole book!" he says in frustration. Exactly.

He's smart like his mother because he goes right for the words she's taught him. On the first page, he picks out ones he's memorized from his nightly note cards. He calls them out like they're stars in the sky. "A. And. At. Be. But. Can. Did. Have. If. Me. My. On. To. Two." We count up the words together. There's a tiny discrepancy between father and son.

" 'A' is not really a word," I try to explain.

"But it is a sound!" he corrects me with a wink. I grab him and we start wrestling on his bed. Then I kiss him all over his face and neck. Not because he's right, but because he's so damn cute. He always has been.

As we fall off the bed laughing together onto the floor, he asks if we can be done for the night.

"Yes, we can be done for the night, Big Man." Baby steps, right? I give him fourteen pennies from a jar I keep in my closet. The same closet I failed him in. The minute I leave his room, I'm sure he grabs the calculator from his backpack and figures out the exact amount he has to go: thirty-six thousand minus fourteen equals just thirty-five thousand, nine hundred, and eighty-six.

The rest of the week we meet every night at the same time in his bedroom. We start learning the sounds together the same way I did with Elvira, Anne Marie, and Melvin. We assign particular words that he likes to each letter of the alphabet.

Words that will hopefully trigger a particular sound whenever he sees that particular letter. Kids love to use words they're not supposed to use. Potty words. It seems to give them some kind of rush like when they eat too much candy. Normally, Andi and I try to keep certain language from entering the front door of our home. When it comes to Oliver's reading, however, all bets are off and some profanity is allowed. His list goes something like this:

A= ass

B= boobies

S= s—t

And yes, when it comes to the sixth letter of the alphabet, I even let him lean in and quietly launch me an F-bomb.

Over the course of the next three weeks, we work together every night. I'm not sure what's driving this runaway locomotive, but Oliver is catching on. Still no official "reading" yet other than the Dolch sight words he has already committed to memory, but he's saying almost every sound correctly. And what seems to be working on the ninth floor in the heart of a historical downtown building with three perfect strangers seems to be working in the second-floor bedroom in the heart of a boy I love more than anything in this world. We go from 14 pennies that first Monday night to 89 pennies on Wednesday to 133 on Friday to 197 on Sunday. Poor Mr. Scary Clown's green eyes are bulging out more than ever, and his swollen belly makes him look like he's four months pregnant.

CHAPTER 15

About this same time, my class at the literacy center is likewise making real progress. We start learning the Dolch list and committing those 220 words to memory. I also print out and photocopy page forty-seven of my copy of the *Tutoring Manual*, which lists an additional 300 or so of the most frequently used words in the English language, also designated as sight words.

They're everywhere: newspapers, magazines, job applications, train and bus schedules, and menus. They occur so often that the act of reading becomes vastly easier just by knowing them. Remember, half of learning to read is based solely on memorization.

The other half is phonics and/or sounding out. Once again, mastering the 300 sight words is important because half of them are phonetically irregular. In other words, we can't figure them out using the trigger words and phrases we have come up with together. For example, the word "of" is pronounced "uv," yet if Anne Marie tries using one of our rules to trigger her memory on how to decode the particular sound (short 'u' equals never look "up"), she'll pronounce it incorrectly. So instead, she must know it. She must memorize it. She must own it.

The key to learning sight words is to do it slowly because teaching long lists of words all at the same time can get boring and frustrating. One word at a time . . . Baby steps.

Here's just a small sample:

the has also day high
going need of when
did same upon look
four and who many
another school asked

within to will before
know every later felt
more must

As we gradually plow through the nearly 300 words, the three students can't believe how many of them they immediately recognize. "I know that one. And that one. And that one. And that one," Elvira happily exclaims.

Melvin starts his own catalog. "Government. Service. Different. Several. But. These. State. House. Hand. Man. There's a ton of words I know."

Anne Marie also realizes many are familiar to her.

After that, I stress how they need to concentrate on the things in life they know, not on the things they don't know.

Society spends so much time telling people—especially adults who can't read and learning-challenged youths—what they don't know that those who are trying to improve their reading skills forget to celebrate what they do. For instance, all the hundreds and hundreds of words they see every day. In red highlighter, I draw the shape of a stop sign on the whiteboard and write the word *stop* inside of it.

"Anne Marie, what's that word say?"

She screams out, "*Stop*!"

"How do you know that?"

"I just do. I know it because I see it every day. I see it when I'm on the bus and when I'm walking on the street to work, and there's one on the corner right across the street from our house next to the grocery store where my dad and I buy our lottery ticket every Tuesday night."

"Exactly. You know it because you've seen it ten thousand times. You own that freaking sign!"

At the end of class, I read an excerpt from the passage in my *Tutoring Manual* regarding the importance of teaching sight words. "Learning these is important because approximately 50 percent of frequently used words in our everyday speech are made up of words found in these lists."

"Hey," broke in Melvin, "that means we're almost halfway home."

Elvira and Anne Marie sit silently smiling back at him. For the first time since we began, I think the threesome begin to believe reading is no longer their impossible dream.

CHAPTER 16

Harold has been coming to Literacy Chicago for almost as long as it's been open. Everybody knows Harold. He's the face of the center. Whether sitting on the sofa in the lobby trying to navigate his way through a page of *Popular Mechanics* or waiting to be summoned by some member of the faculty to help in any small way he can, Harold is always present.

He never misses orientation Wednesday. Ever. He arrives early to write all of the pertinent information on the blackboard for the school's newest students. Nobody else would think of performing this task because everyone knows it's Harold's job. Whenever you enter the classroom, you'll know exactly where, when, and why you are there. Just glance at the board. Harold's board.

WEDNESDAY. 3:00 PM. ORIENTATION. WELCOME.

I can't explain exactly why this simple act of recording this simple information on a blackboard by this sixty-something-year-old little man melts my heart; it just does. The pride he takes in doing so is indescribable. And at the end of every session, dutiful Harold attentively erases this same information to leave the premises he presides over clean and ready for a new day. I should also mention that Harold's reading level is not quite that of a second-semester first grader. Although his efforts to improve are unequalled, his retention fades as quickly as the chalk on his board.

Ironically, Harold looks a great deal like another tender man I once was privileged to have in my life. Kids always choose different pet names for their grandparents. I picked "Poppie." He was the one who first got me interested in baseball. Poppie knew all the players on the Chicago Cubs: their positions, their numbers, and their stats. And whenever I visited him at his job, he tested me to make sure I had been listening. I soon knew the complete batting order of the Cubs from top to bottom and every single statistic you can imagine, no matter how trivial.

He was a florist. Actually, he worked as an assistant to the florist in a small suburban store, watering the flowers and carrying in heavy bags of fertilizer and dirt. Though he weighed about 135 pounds, to me he was Hercules. And I sure hated how his boss talked to him. "Leonard, are those bags of manure going to carry themselves up the stairs?" I learned what manure was when I rode a pony for the first time. (It was at the very same place I took Isabella and Oliver some thirty-five years later.) I didn't think my Poppie should have to carry it on his back.

But my Poppie didn't teach me only about hard work, humility, and baseball. This slight, undereducated fertilizer schlepper helped me learn to read. Of course, like any other kid starting school, I was learning the basics. But he made sure I practiced. On Saturdays we would read from the back of baseball cards. Words like: Batting Average. Home Runs. Stolen Bases. Singles. Doubles. Triples. Strikeouts. Innings. Games. Those were just some of my "Dolch" words. We also read from the backs of flower seed packets, the small ones that would be set up on display cases in the front of the florist shop next to the cash register. I learned to read directions in small print about how to grow certain flowers: how many seeds to use and how deep to plant them. By the age of eight, I could have landed a job at any nursery in the country.

He was a simple man, my Poppie. We would take long walks around his block and talk about nothing. And everything. He liked me just because I was his grandson. Sometimes when I was in high school I would walk two miles to visit him at the nursing home when nobody else could take me. He was in the advanced stages of Alzheimer's, and most of the time he was angry, delusional, and completely out of it. But occasionally, when I'd bring some old baseball cards to look at or I'd ask when I should plant a pumpkin seed so it would arrive just in time for Halloween, he'd be the old Poppie I knew and loved so well.

Today after Anne Marie, Elvira, Melvin, and I finish class, there is a note from Aunt June Porter waiting for me at the front desk. At first I think I've done something wrong. It feels like I am being summoned to the principal's office. I wait to open it until I step into the elevator.

Dear Rob,

You are doing a good job. I've decided to add another student to your group. Hope that's okay.

June.
P.S. How's Oliver?

The next time I walk into class, the first thing I notice is the writing on the blackboard.

WEDNESDAY. 4:00 PM. ROB'S CLASS. WELCOME.

Sitting proudly in the first row next to Melvin, chalk residue on his fingertips, is my new student, Harold. The ghost of Poppie.

CHAPTER 17

One of the words we dissected on the blackboard a few weeks ago was COINCIDENCE. That's what we call breaking up a word. Dissecting. Like a big juicy frog. The bigger the word, the juicier the frog. We also call it "digging for treasure" because every new word we learn together is like finding a shiny pearl.

"Remember," I remind the class, "concentrate on what you do know, not what you don't. Find a word inside the word."

Let the hunting begin. Melvin pulls out the "CO," which he recognizes from "co-op" and "companies." Companies like the ones over the years who never hired him or gave him a chance because he couldn't read. Up next is Elvira, identifying "IN." On deck, Anne Marie, who loves watching her favorite reality shows every night, sitting on the couch with her dad in their "DEN." She's particularly fond of *Fear Factor*. She can't believe someone would truly swallow a live grasshopper. She remembers catching them in paper cups with her cousin when she was a little girl.

Two heads are better than one. Four are even stronger. For now, Harold sits back and observes. We have COIN__ DEN__. That's seven out of eleven letters. More than halfway home. It's not always that easy, however. A CI-gar is not always a cigar. Why a C followed by an I, E, or Y magically changes its sound from a "K" as in CAT to an "S" as in CENT is hard for them to grasp. But creating some useful tricks can help. When people hear the word *tricks* they automatically think of the act of cheating. Anne Marie is CEO of that noble corporation.

"Rob, James 4:17," she softly offers.

"Huh?"

"The Bible says whoever knows the right thing to do and fails to do it, for him it is a sin." She brings up her copy of the black book previously lounging peacefully in her JoAnn Fabrics sewing bag.

"I'm not suggesting we cheat, Annie," the lawyer in me says, determined to set the record straight. "In fact, cheating will never get us to Canaan." She smiles. "When I say 'tricks,' I mean shortcuts." Her smile disappears. "I don't exactly mean shortcuts." I'm perspiring as if trapped inside the confessional box. "There are ways to help us memorize things we need to know to keep improving our reading. Small clues that help us with our treasure map." The smile is back—and the good book returns to its resting place.

I grab a marker and draw a picture of a treasure chest. Scribbles representing rubies and other jewels are hanging off the sides. Inside the chest I start writing whatever comes into my head. ING. TION. E's and Y's at the end of a word such as coffeE and daisY. EA. OA. EE. OO. ER. IR. UR. AR. As I write I call out, "Hey, Melvin. You take two trains, two buses, and about two hundred steps to get here, right?" Melvin nods. "What if I told you there was a way for you to only have to take one train, one bus, and one hundred steps, getting you here in half the time. Would you do it?"

"Hell, yeah," he says. I notice Anne Marie quickly reaching toward her sewing bag.

"Apologize, Melvin," I admonish.

"Sorry, my dear." (Lately, Melvin has been using the phrase "my dear" a lot whenever he's speaking to Anne Marie. "Good afternoon, my dear. Have a nice night, my dear. Pass the Doritos, my dear." A knight wooing the damsel in distress. Strangers quickly become united, held together by a single common thread.)

"But wait a second, Melvin. Isn't that cheating?" I ask.

"Hell no . . . sorry. No, it is not cheating. It just gets me here quicker."

"Exactly! And that's what I mean by memorizing some of these little shortcuts. It gets us to learn a word quicker."

I point to the shin on my left foot. Every time they see the TION at the end of a word, they will think of me pointing at my shin and remember that's the sound this ending makes. SHIN. And when they see a word that ends with ING, they will think of Mr. T—Elvira's favorite movie star—and remember all of the bling-bling he wears around his neck.

When they see the letters A and R together, AR, I want them to immediately think of what a pirate says. I make everyone cover one of their eyes with their palm and together, doing our best Blackbeard impersonations, we bellow out "ARRRRRRRR!"

Then I tell them a joke. "A rabbi, a priest, and a minister walk into a bar . . ." It's an awful joke. I get three pity laughs and a half-hearted smirk from Harold. But it helps me introduce the next topic: Namely, what happens when you have two vowels together in the middle of a word? "The E and the A get all gussied up to go out dancing at the club. Before they walk in, E turns around to A and says, 'Hey, Bub, when we get in there, let me do all the talking.' In other words, when you see two vowels together, the first one does the talking, and the second one is the wingman: lEAf. bOAt. tAIl."

The point of our lesson that evening is that some things are just more difficult to learn than others. Making these obstacles silly and fun helps us, in the long run, to retain them more easily. Since then, during every class, we add more and more tricks to our list, which is sectioned off on the right side of the whiteboard. As always, Harold continues to keep his board spotless at the end of each class but now leaves the "tricked out" side of it proudly in plain view for all to see.

At the top of the list, in electric pink letters, is a famous quote from Walt Disney:

> "There is more treasure in books than in all the pirates' loot on Treasure Island."

CHAPTER 18

"How would you like that broken up?" Yolanda asks as she takes the crisp one-hundred-dollar bill from inside the plastic tube. She's the cute junior teller at the drive-thru window at my bank.

"In pennies," I answer.

"Excuse me, in what?" she exclaims.

"Um, pennies. I'd like that in pennies, please." There's a pause. Long enough for me to know she thinks I'm some kind of juvenile practical joker.

"Are you kidding, sir?"

"No, really. I need a hundred dollars in pennies." I truly do. Oliver is a penny junkie, and we are all out of our stash at home. Six hundred, seven hundred, eight hundred a night.

And he has developed his own storage system: five blue plumber's plastic buckets he found in the basement, left over from last year when we had to funnel out sewer water after the historic spring flood.

I hear Yolanda's voice—"One second, please"—trailing off as she gets up from her chair and walks away from the window. A few minutes later her supervisor's voice comes over the speaker asking me to come inside the bank. I pull around into the parking lot and get out of my car. Ten minutes later, with the help of the Barney Fife security guard, I've loaded eight cardboard boxes, filled with ten thousand pennies, into my backseat.

One of the main obstacles still standing in Oliver's way of becoming a legitimate and bona fide reader is his inability to get from point A to point B to point C. In other words, even though he knows the entire Dolch list by heart and has mastered every single sound of the alphabet, including every possible blend and combination of different letters, he is still having difficulty joining everything together. He is excellent at the task of breaking down a word into several different pieces, though. For example, here's how he tackles the word EXPLANATION.

EX (like the X-ray he had at the hospital last summer after cutting open his chin).

PL (like the word *please*, which he learned works a whole lot better than "Give me that damn Popsicle now!").

AN (one of his sight words).

A (as in the sound he used to beat me out of a penny that first night on page one of *Black Beauty*).

And finally TION (as in SHIN, the first four letters of his last name).

The problem isn't dissecting the word. It is putting everything back together and stretching the individual sounds out to form one.

That's where Flick Park comes in. Flick Park is the place where I spent almost every day of every summer growing up as a kid. It had a baseball field with a home-run fence and its own scoreboard. A concession stand with foot-long hot dogs for eighty-nine cents. And an Olympic-size pool, which Marty the maintenance man, who had only three fingers on his left hand, kept at over eighty degrees. But it was also the only pool within a fifty-mile radius that had a diving board. Actually, there were three diving boards. High. Higher. And Highest. It took nearly four years of dares, double dares, and super-duper triple dares to finally coax me up to the top of number three, which we all called Jupiter because when you stood at its edge and looked down, it seemed like you were in outer space.

On a muggy Thursday night in May, we take Isabella, Oliver, Sage, and a few of their friends to Flick Park for a night of fun. It's still a popular suburban hangout and looks just the same. The concession stand is still open, but the foot-longs have been replaced by eight-bucks-apiece pygmy Red Hots. As I watch Oliver jump off the diving board (there are only two now; Jupiter was retired upon the advice of overly cautious insurance companies), I get an idea. Not being able to put all the respective sounds of a word together is like not being able to take that final plunge off the high dive. To step to the edge and just fall forward.

So the next day we go back to Flick. Just the two of us. It is early, and only a few teenagers are lying on lawn chairs, smoking cigarettes, and working on their tans. Oliver and I climb up the metal stairs together—I with my copy of *Black Beauty* in hand and Oliver wearing his sixty-five-dollar swimming goggles.

As we stand at the top of the board, I pick out a word on the page and Oliver dissects it, breaking it into individual sounds as he did in his bedroom. Then he places his toes over the edge of the board, looks down, and after a few moments of taunting and super-duper triple daring from his father, he closes his eyes and jumps. As he falls, I yell out the word, holding its echo until his body hits the water and then pops back up to the surface. It reminds me of the last sounds I hear after screaming greetings into the bottom of a canyon. Sometimes my comedic genius son intentionally stays under a few extra seconds just to see how long I can hold the note. On the word *sympathy* I think I might even pass out.

After a dozen or so trips up and down those stairs, Oliver takes over the role as yodeler. I point to a word, we say it out loud together, and then he jumps. As he leaps off the board, he screams at the top of his lungs, holding different parts of each word—beginnings, middles, and ends—while he soars through the air.

SentimentALLLLLL. SaDDDDDDle. CarriaGGGGGE. TranspoPORRRTAAAtion. AboLLLishmeNNTT. I HAAAte YoUUUUU DAAAAAADDDD!

That morning my son scales up and down the stairs of that diving board so many times the bottom of his feet begin to blister. He does regular dives. Belly flops. Cannonballs. But by the time he sits his crinkly butt back onto the cool leather seat of the car, somehow it has clicked. He begins understanding how to stretch individual sounds of a word together. He is officially reading. And I am officially bankrupt. The next morning I notice Yolanda leave to take her break early when she sees me pull up to the drive-through window.

CHAPTER 19

My recent breakthrough on the home front with Oliver is mirrored by the progress being made by my quartet at Literacy Chicago. At first glance, to the untrained eye, the students at the center may not exactly entice someone's desire to believe they have value. In fact, that's been the problem during most of their lives. But when you take your time, look closer, and investigate, you see that there is worth. Something that is beautiful. Something that is real. A diamond in the rough, so to speak.

After Harold joins the class, his presence lifts everyone to a different level. Although he reads at a first-grade level, he speaks like a prophet. And even though I never met Moses, I somehow imagine this is just how he would have looked. Dignified, hair completely gray. Dark, soulful eyes. Endowed with a reassuring calmness that makes you feel safe in his presence. Yes, it is as if Moses has come down from the mountain again, holding tablets upon which is written the message of life for those of us in that classroom.

One day it occurs to me my students know why I called Literacy Chicago, but I don't know what drove them to come here. I ask each of the four of them in turn. I let Harold go first. After pausing to think about what he wants to say, remaining seated with a sense of propriety, he begins.

"I always worked really hard. I got my first job when I was twelve helping my uncle clean buildings. It was never hard for me to work. I liked it. It made me feel good. Soon I had another job. And then another. I always had four or five jobs. I love taking something that's dirty and making it clean. It's not that I didn't want to go to school. It just never seemed to be the right time."

Harold pauses a moment and reaches over to grab a handful of M&M's from the bag on Anne Marie's desk. (Lately, Anne Marie has been supplying the entire class with different weekly treats.) After reflecting for a few seconds, he continues.

"Before I knew it, I was a grown man who couldn't read. But I was earning good money from all the working I was doing. And my wife was a really smart lady and she did all the reading for us. But then she died, so nobody was there to help me anymore. And at the end of every month, I'd have to give most of my money away to people who would do the things she used to do. Like the person who helped me pay my bills.

Or the one who read me my mail. So then I realized a few years ago that I had spent my whole life doing what everybody else wanted me to do. I decided it was time to do something that I wanted to do. And what I wanted to do was keep my own money. So I heard about this place and I came to see Miss June Porter. Now I pay my own bills."

"Thanks, Harold. Okay, Miss E. Your turn."

At first she's reluctant, as she'd been in those first few classes, when you couldn't get her mouth to grin even if you'd used a crowbar. "Let Melvin go first," she tries to negotiate.

"Nope. Beauty before the Giant," I say. They both smile. And then Elvira's story comes pouring out as if she's untangled a garden hose.

"It was domestic battery." She hesitates. Harold gently places his hand on her shoulder. It is the first time I notice his ring. He wears it on his pinky, but the onyx stone on top almost covers the entire finger. I remember my grandfather having a similar ring. Elvira exhales and pushes on.

"It was domestic battery that brought me here. It happened for a lot of years. I couldn't leave because of my son. He was special and he needed me to be around. His father . . . well, his father had a lot of problems in his life. For a long time, I was frozen inside. I stopped learning. I forgot everything I knew. After he died, I didn't want to be frozen anymore so I came here. To get unfrozen." Anne Marie affectionately offers Elvira some caramel corn, but she politely declines while wiping off the lenses of her glasses.

"All right, grocery store lady, it's your turn." I already know Anne Marie's and Melvin's stories from orientation Wednesdays, but I still want to hear them again.

Anne Marie reaches down into her JoAnn Fabrics sewing bag and brings up her Bible. She takes hold of it with both hands and holds it against her chest for a moment or two. Then she extends it out, turns it around to look at its front, and ceremoniously places it back down into the sewing bag. Right next to her Fritos.

"You all thought I was going to say I'm here because of my Bible. That I want to learn to read so I can read the Bible. But that ain't true. I already can read the Bible. Because I heard the priest read it so many times I almost have all the important parts already memorized. Oh sure, I want to learn how to read the other parts. But that ain't what brought me here. My mama brought me here. Before she died, she always kept wanting me to be good in school. I hated school. I hated my teachers, I hated gym, and I hated all those tiny little girls who made fun of how big my feet were. They called me 'Anne Man Feet.' When my mama died, I couldn't even help my daddy write out what we wanted to say in the church bulletin. And then I couldn't even read what he and my auntie wrote down.

"But now, my cousin is about to graduate high school and go off to college. Every night after dinner and cleaning off the table, she and Daddy would sit on the couch and read their horoscopes together. My mama was a Capricorn, so they'd read hers too. Just to see how she was making out up in heaven. When my cousin's gone, it will be just me and my daddy in the house. And he won't have anyone to read his and Mama's horoscopes with anymore. That's why I am here." She reaches down and picks out a handful of Fritos and places them in her mouth. Then she takes a sip from her Big Gulp.

Last but not least is Melvin. Over the last few months, his size has grown even larger. Not physically speaking, but emotionally. He's always the first one to arrive in the room and the last one on the elevator. After class he sits around in the lobby and talks to whoever will listen. It's not that he has no place to go. That's not it. I think he just likes how the place feels on him. He's making more progress than perhaps he ever thought he could, and even when we're not sitting in class dissecting words listed on the blackboard, I think he believes that being on the premises will somehow keep filling him up with knowledge.

"All right, Melvin, bring us all home," I say.

"Short and sweet, that's all I can say."

Initially, I think he means that's what his answer to the question is going to be. Melvin is a man of few words. Few and deep. But he is actually referring to his daughter, Allanna. She's in the fifth grade, and this is the first time any of us has ever heard about her. After all, Melvin seemed to be a professional bachelor. Six months after Allanna was born, her mother disappeared. Melvin raised Allanna on his own, and now that she is a schoolgirl, a nice neighbor looks in on her after school before Melvin gets home from work and tutoring. I can't imagine any offspring procreated by Melvin would be short in stature, but Melvin says she's "as teeny as a tulip." In fact, that's what he calls her, "Tulip," and she's the reason he comes down to 17 North State Street to the literacy center.

"You know that show on television *Are You Smarter Than a 5th Grader?*" he asks. "Well, I know the answer. I'm not. And I'm not as smart as a fourth grader or a third grader or a second grader. And I couldn't even help her when she started kindergarten. And it didn't seem all that important because she knew I loved her. But now, for some reason, that doesn't seem enough. She wants to go to the Harold Washington Library and enter the school history fair and win a trip down to Springfield to see the state capitol. And I can't even read the entry application. She may not be embarrassed by her daddy, but her daddy is embarrassed by her daddy. So that's why I'm here. To be able to take my little girl to the library and not wait out in the car in the parking lot."

Anne Marie offers him some chips. At first, he refuses. Then he grabs hold of the bag and says, "Thanks, Annie, my dear."

Take your time, look closer, and investigate. If you do, you may just find a diamond. Or two . . . or three . . . or four . . .

CHAPTER 20

At the start of the next class, Aunt June Porter stops me before I begin and asks if she can see me for a moment. I feel a flash of apprehension pass through my insides.

Maybe she heard how we spent last session in "church" rather than reading. After all, on the first day of the tutoring seminar, one of the speakers specifically advised us to maintain a safe and professional distance from our students. No intimate personal information was to be shared in class. And for a while I maintained such a distance, but relationships develop organically, and it's impossible to keep your distance when hearts are opened and stakes are raised to such a high level at such an intense pace.

Turns out, though, June isn't upset. Quite the opposite. A few tutors had recently dropped out and she needed a home for some new students who had just begun the program.

Would I be willing to increase my class size? she asks. You just don't say "no" to Aunt June Porter. At least I don't. Ever. Remember, a few weeks ago, Oliver Perlis Shindler had leaped off suburbia's highest diving board screaming four-syllable words from page 114 of *Black Beauty*. That would never, ever have happened if I hadn't found Aunt June Porter. So no, I never say "no" to Aunt June.

The only dilemma with adding new students to the class is that, per my original pledge regarding how elephants travel, nobody moves forward unless we all move forward. Together. Therefore, we must start over again. From the very beginning. Letters of the alphabet. Vowels. Consonants. Blends. The Dolch list. Everything. Luckily, the four "veteran" students currently enlisted under my tutelage respect the process and can't be more understanding and eager to help. "Baby steps, right?" says Anne Marie.

That afternoon, three new students join our troupe. Two women and a man. A mirror of our initial threesome. But unlike the first trio, these three are almost exact opposites. Instead of being gigantic like Melvin, Michael is miniature. And from the very first words out of his mouth, I can tell Michael is anything but jolly. He is like vinegar. He doesn't want to be here and he has no problem making sure I know that. As a condition to the disposition in his case, a "racist judge" (Michael's word, not mine) ordered him to register at the center. So my new male student's lone motivation is basically to stay out of jail. One more thing you should know about Michael. He is in a wheelchair and is missing both legs up to the knees.

Next to Michael is Edna. For some reason, I've recently noticed that the people in this world who have everything—money, the big house, education, degrees—every reason on the planet to smile, don't. And the people walking around this earth with much, much less, smile much, much more. Is it ignorance, or do they know something we don't? I can't help being reminded of this contradiction the moment Edna speaks. As she stands to introduce herself, she clears her throat like a first grader does right before addressing her classmates at the start of the school year. With the fingers of her left hand, she carefully smoothes down the crease on the same dress I'm certain she wore just a few days before at Sunday's services in the House of the Lord.

She is serious about being here, evidenced by both her choice in wardrobe and her demeanor. But just as it has been with Melvin, Anne Marie, and ultimately Elvira, it is her smile that burns a permanent imprint in my mind. And right smack in the center of that beaming grin is a gold tooth the size of the letter T on your computer keyboard. It is shiny and bright and, even when you try, you can't take your eyes off it while she talks. And similar to Anne Marie, Edna totes a knitting bag with her. As she stores it on the floor under her chair, I see balls of colored yarn, needles, and the start of a pink sweater or scarf she obviously has been working on for some time.

Finishing up the group is Gail. Quiet and reserved. Although her smile is not as openly apparent as Edna's, I sense an immediate warmth from Gail and know she feels comfortable in her new surroundings. Before we start attacking the vowels of the alphabet, Gail wants me to know up front that she suffers from sickle cell anemia and occasionally will be missing class to go to a variety of doctor's appointments.

As in every other class in the past, the first thing we do is run through the alphabet. "How do athletes warm up before they take the field before a big game?" I ask the group.

Without raising his hand, Michael yells out, "They cash their big f—in' paycheck and smoke a big f—in' joint."

"No, Michael, that's what gang members do before a big game. Athletes stretch. They exercise." He rolls his eyes and the wheels on his chair back and forth. "And how does Whitney Houston get ready before a concert?"

Edna raises her hand. "Go ahead, Miss Edna," I say.

"Ms. Whitney don't need any practice." Everybody laughs. "But I guess if she did, she would practice all her notes and warm up that beautiful voice the Almighty gave her."

"That's right," I agree. "So we need to do the same. Like an athlete or famous diva, we need to warm up and exercise before we read." I write the vowels on the blackboard. Michael begins pulling at one of the stickers on the handles of his chair. I can't exactly make it out, but I think one of the graphics is of a topless woman wearing a bandana.

After putting A – E – I – O – U up on the board, underneath the letters I write out "MCHL." The three new students look puzzled. Michael just looks angry and bored. Anne Marie, Elvira, and Melvin know exactly what's going on.

I walk over to Michael and hold out my hand. After a few grueling seconds, he reluctantly extends his and we shake. He's wearing two leather gloves like a baseball player or weightlifter would to protect his hands. "Has everyone met my friend MCHL?" I ask. The word comes out sounding like a backward hiccup. He looks up at me like he's planning my funeral. I return to the board and add the missing letters. "Without the 'i' and the 'a' and the 'e' we don't have the name his parents gave him. But with the vowels, we have our Michael."

"F— my parents!" he says. I remind him not to forget to pick up a card for Father's Day next week.

To say Michael would be a challenge over the next few weeks would be an understatement.

In case you haven't noticed, Michael is a huge fan of the F-bomb. Even during his brief thirty-second introduction to the class he drops four or five missiles. And we quickly learn there is to be no cease-fire after that. If he misses the sound of a vowel on the board . . . F-bomb. If I accidentally call on someone out of turn when he's raising his hand . . . F-bomb. If the fly in the room unintentionally lands on the tire of his wheelchair . . . F-bomb.

But this guy can learn. He says he doesn't, but he does. I notice this right from the start. And every time he tosses out another grenade, you can hear the dual shrieks in stereo coming from Anne Marie and Edna sitting in the front row. Edna, unlike Anne Marie, may not carry her Bible in her sewing bag, but after meeting Michael, I'm sure she wishes she had.

One time during class I hear Michael whisper to the person sitting next to him, "How the f— is this f—in' white boy gonna teach us anything?" It is the first time that fact hits me. Not that I *am* a "f—in' white boy," mind you, but that I am the only white boy. The only light-skinned person in the room. This reality is not a new revelation to me: On that first elevator ride with Melvin, I knew he was black and I wasn't black. When I first said hello to Anne Marie and Elvira, I knew they weren't white. And I knew Harold was African American. I was well aware of the differences between my students and me, but it never, ever seemed to matter. Until that moment.

I suddenly realize Michael probably sees me as the guy on the other side of the fence, dressed as I am in my lawyerly suit and tie every day. The one who couldn't possibly understand him and, therefore, couldn't possibly help him. I know BS-ing him is definitely not the way to win him over. So until I can show him what I am made of on the inside, I decide I have to start with what he sees on the outside.

The very next day I put a change of clothes in a gym bag I leave in my car. Before every class thereafter, I get undressed in the backseat and slip into my sweatshirt, blue jeans, and Converse high tops. I feel like Clark Kent inside a telephone booth changing from one uniform into another. What really makes me feel like some kind of superhero, though, is what I am accomplishing in my little classroom at the literacy center.

I understand that if we are going to survive together without Anne Marie and Edna going into cardiac arrest over Michael's bleep-bleep-bleeping, I have to get his language at least a little under control. But I suspect the whole quarter-in-a-jar routine isn't going to work. So I come up with another idea. Every time he drops an F-bomb, he has to give me five. Not dollars or push-ups, but words. Words that I choose from the dictionary. Michael has to sound them out, break them down, and figure them out. When he succeeds, I put a quarter in the vase sitting on the back table next to the globe. We start calling the process "Michael's Lemonade Stand."

We agree that at the end of every month we will empty the winnings from the vase and take a field trip to the Starbucks on the corner. Turns out, Michael's devoted infatuation with the letter F allows everyone in class to enjoy the java of their choice.

After our third session together, Gail wants to know the name of our class.

"What do you mean *our* name?" I ask.

"Yeah, our name. What do we call ourselves? I tell all the people at the day care center about me going to school and they ask me what's the name of our class?"

"Well, I guess it's 'Beginning Reading.' How about 'Phonics'?"

She doesn't like either of those. "No, not that. I mean, what do we call ourselves? Like some schools are the Tigers or the Wolves. My cousin goes to school in South Carolina and they're known as the Gamecocks." Everyone laughs, even Michael. I can't help noticing Anne Marie's hand curling up around her Bible. I know Gail is as innocent as a preschooler and has no idea what she just tossed across the bow. You can sense, however, Michael has gained a newfound respect for her.

"Okay, okay. I get it. You want to come up with a nickname for us, right? That's a great idea. Any suggestions?"

A few shout out some generic ideas. We R Readers. Rob's Readers. Seven in Heaven. Finally Gail suggests we use the first letter of every person's first name to make one big word.

"I think that's an unbelievable idea, Gail. Unbelievable. Certainly better than the Gamecocks. The name we form by using those letters is called an acronym."

"I saw this great movie about that a long time ago about these big f—in' spiders that were taking over the whole state. It was f—in' unbelievable!" says Michael.

I carefully correct him. "I think you may mean Arachnophobia. Which means fear of spiders."

"Yeah, I knew that." I think he did.

We all agree that G should go first because, after all, it was Gail's idea. On the board, I write the first letter of the first name of everyone else. Then I cross out the duplicates: E for Elvira and Edna and M for Melvin and Michael. I place the A for Anne Marie at the beginning (ladies first) and an H at the caboose for Harold. As I back away from the board, I can't believe it. Nor could I possibly have planned it. I'm not sure God could have. But together smack in the middle we get the word GEM. As in diamonds. And emeralds. And rubies. I remember learning a lot about diamonds when I was shopping for an engagement ring. I learned every diamond is different. I also learned no two stones are the same. All are beautiful and precious and valuable. But they are also all flawed in some way. Like the people sitting in front of me, and like their tutor sitting in front of them. Whether it is destiny, a coincidence, or just dumb luck, no other choice is possible for the name of our class. We will forever be known as the GEMS.

Harold stands up, walks to the blackboard, and with the stick of chalk he always carries in his pocket, he erases the A and the H and relocates the two letters underneath the word GEMS. Only this time, he lists them in reverse order: H, A.

"What's that?" I ask.

In his soft southern voice, he answers, "The H is for Harold and the A is for Anne Marie." He points to the door. "And what do we say when someone out there says we can't learn to read?"

Without waiting for a reaction, he blurts out his own answer. "We say HA! Ha, ha, ha, ha, ha, ha, ha!"

The room roars, everyone joining in, and I'm almost certain you could hear the ha, ha, ha, haing at the jewelry store on Madison Avenue five blocks away.

CHAPTER 21

My mother may have given me life, but my second-grade teacher, Mrs. Imergluck, was the first female who made me feel *alive*. And even though I knew she was happily married and almost twenty years my senior, I was still confident we had a future together.

Fast-forward thirty-six years. I see the same blaze in his eyes whenever Oliver speaks of his own Mrs. Imergluck, whom he met on the first Tuesday of his fifth-grade year. And I see it in the way he picks out his clothes the night before school, making absolutely certain everything matches perfectly. Even his socks. His walk is even different: He bounces. Mrs. Hughes (happily married and more than twenty years older) makes Oliver feel like a billion bucks. Like he's special. Not that kind of special. The other *special*. Like he matters. Like he can leap tall buildings in a single bound. The way a teacher should make you feel.

Mrs. Hughes voluntarily starts a reading program after school in her classroom for kids who are having trouble. No extra pay or benefits. Five kids sign up. Jeremy, Fernanda, Justin, Amber, and Oliver. I ask if I can help. (Don't forget, in case I have not mentioned it, I'm a certified reading tutor at this point!)

Mrs. Hughes is grateful to have the help. Her only advice for me is to make sure I treat Oliver like any other student.

So every Tuesday afternoon from 2:15 to 3:00, I become Mrs. Hughes's assistant. But something playing well in one venue doesn't mean it will work in another. The five grade-schoolers hate my teaching method. I may be a big hit on State Street when I use silly little rhymes or sayings with Anne Marie, Elvira, and the others, but Oliver's classmates aren't buying into it. They laugh at me—and not in a good way. If Oliver could have rubbed two shiny pennies together, blinked his eyes, and transported himself into another stratosphere, he would have!

The night after my first visit with Mrs. Hughes's Fab Five, we're sitting together on the couch in the family room watching TV. Well, Oliver's watching; I'm once again trying to discover exactly where he's hidden the remote. I may have bought that flat screen, but he clearly owns it. *That's So Raven* is on. The cute little girl from *The Cosby Show* is all grown up and remarkably even more annoying on her own show. Oliver knows every single line before the words fall off each actor's lips. He's memorized the entire thirty minutes, including the commercials! Suddenly a lightbulb goes off in my head. The next morning, I call Walt Disney Productions in Florida. After being transferred nine different times, I finally speak with Joy and explain my crazy idea. Two days later, a copy of the actual transcript from one of their episodes arrives in the mail. The following Tuesday, I try something a little different with the Fab Five. No silly rhymes or catchy sayings. Just . . . *action*!

Jeremy plays Raven. He insists! Oliver is Corey, the wacky brother. Justin is the mischievous, kooky friend. Amber and Fernanda star in supporting roles. As the director, I quickly remind them there are no small parts, only small actors. They love it. And truth be told, Jeremy is Emmy Award worthy in the role of Raven. A few weeks later, I receive another transcript. And then another. Soon we almost have our own sitcom. Turns out, they're all hams, especially Fernanda, who initially could barely be heard. But it's working. They're becoming better readers. Mrs. Hughes suggests we try something different. Something a little harder.

The following week I bring in Bill Clinton's autobiography, *My Life*, a birthday gift from my mother-in-law that has been sitting on the nightstand next to my bed for nearly ten months. Nine hundred and seventy-eight pages! Rather than laugh, the kids simply want to initiate impeachment proceedings against me!

"Is your dad out of his mind?" Justin asks Oliver.

I try something that works with my adult students. The theory behind baby steps. Only instead of using the whole African elephant adaptation of togetherness and grabbing onto tails as we cross the desert, I try a variation on the swing dance Snowball.

"Ooohh," shrieks Amber, "I'm not dancing with any of them."

I assure her no one needs to boogie. Instead, we all sit in a circle and Jeremy starts to read. After six words, I yell out "snowball," which means he's to pass the book off to Fernanda. Six more words and it's Oliver's turn. And so on and so on. Soon, everyone wants more and more time on the dance floor and complains when it's their turn to pass off the ever-larger "snowball."

In a little more than fourteen Tuesdays, we plow through just forty-two pages. But if you ask Justin how President Clinton's dad died, he'll tell you it happened in a car accident one week before little Bill was born. How the police found Mr. Clinton in a pond with his outstretched hand clenching a branch, which he had used to try and pull himself out of the water to save himself. That's how much he wanted to see his baby boy come into the world. Ask what twelve-year-old William Jefferson's favorite pastime was in the summer and Amber will recite how, more than anything, he loved hanging out at his grandfather's grocery store stacking shelves. How did he learn to get along with kids of all colors? The Fab Five are a potpourri of black, white, and brown, and they all know the answer. That's just how Bill was raised.

Those forty-two pages help each child realize something. That anybody from anywhere could some day become president. Telling our kids they can leap tall buildings in a single bound is one thing. Introducing them to someone who actually did it is another.

CHAPTER 22

He's a small man, barely five feet tall. He wears his faded blue jeans high, nearly an inch above his belly button, the white fabric of the pockets peeking out like frightened bunny ears. His hair sits on top of his head as if someone simply placed it there like an accessory from Mr. Potato Head. At first glance, most people wouldn't even notice him, and even if they did, he would be quickly categorized as irrelevant. Insignificant. To her, however, he's everything but that.

At any other point in time and in any other place, you wouldn't, you couldn't, possibly picture these two contrasts standing together only inches apart. But today in this room they seem as one. At least thirty years his junior, this statuesque African American woman with a magnificent body and golden brown skin gazes down at him like his face is worthy of being set in granite on Mount Rushmore. And when it's finally her turn to address the audience, she sounds confident and secure.

She explains how they just completed their final session to prepare her for the GED exam. Although she turned twenty-eight the week prior, she had dropped out of school when she was fifteen after becoming pregnant. When they started working side by side a few years earlier, she read at the level of a second grader. They've trekked miles together. And according to her, he has "removed roadblocks from her path."

When she finishes, he begins to speak. He's awkward and uncomfortable. Yet she clings onto every word he says like a newborn baby clutches onto her mother while nursing. She adores this man who to the general public is simply a stranger with a bad hairdo.

He's her tutor. And today the literacy center is presenting him with an award for ten years of service. It's a small gathering in the kitchen, where store-bought cookies and cans of ginger ale are passed out. There's also a pound cake with ten candles on it. When he blows them out, the twenty or so invited guests stand and applaud. Her tutor blushes and looks away toward the microwave. She hands him a pillow her auntie helped her crochet with the following words inscribed on it: "Thank You For Turning My Blank Canvass Into Something I Can Now Paint On." After the GED exam, she hopes to get a job at an accounting office. She loves numbers and would like to help her mom do her own taxes.

When June Porter thanks everyone for coming, the student turns and hugs her tutor with a genuineness that feels like she's just hugged the whole room. I wonder if he realizes how enormous he appears at that very moment to everyone in this room. He's a superhero, and I never even knew his name.

CHAPTER 23

Because of Oliver's learning disability, his twin sister, Isabella—affectionately known as Belly—became a pioneer in helping others. In fourth grade, for example, she began volunteering in the special education classroom at their school. Instead of playing kickball at recess, one or two mornings each week she would help Miss McLain's kids with their reading charts or bring in Sweet Tarts from our candy drawer at home to help them learn how to add and subtract. She is an old soul in a young girl's body.

And that's how Horoscope Wednesday is born. Isabella comes up with the idea a few weeks after I bring her to one of my sessions at the literacy center. They all love her from the start and immediately sense her goodness. They have lots of questions about our family and want to know what I am really like at home. What I look like in the morning, can I dance, and do I ever get angry. Isabella forms an instant bond with Anne Marie.

I'm not sure whether it is their shared love for 7-Eleven Big Gulps or the tub of cotton candy Anne Marie just happens to bring to class that day, but the two hit it off like schoolgirls on the playground.

On the way home in the car, Belly asks me, "Daddy, did you know Anne Marie's daddy reads her her horoscope every night after dinner?"

"Yeah, it's really sweet, isn't it? She lost her mommy a long time ago."

"Yeah, and she has two cats. One's name is Bo-Bo and the other is Carl. And her favorite flavor is Mountain Dew, but the store near her house doesn't have it a lot. So she gets Coke instead."

I am realizing you can learn a whole lot about a person while sharing cotton candy.

"I have an idea, Daddy. Wouldn't it be cool if they could switch?"

"What do you mean 'switch'?" I ask.

"If Anne Marie could read her dad's horoscope to him after dinner!"

As a father, I find it difficult to explain the admiration that floods my entire being as I listen to my baby girl describe how she effortlessly extended herself to a perfect stranger.

The following week I stop off and pick up a newspaper on the way to class. I tear out page forty-nine from the *Sun Times* and toss the rest into the garbage. I arrive fifteen minutes early so I have time to put everything up on the board before the seven students get there. My plan is to start with Anne Marie's horoscope and then we'll work our way through the class list. Girl, boy, girl, boy . . . I'm not sure how it will go over, but if they like the idea we could spend the next month or so reading horoscopes.

Like an unexpected off-Broadway hit, Horoscope Wednesday is a smash. What started as my amazing little girl's brainstorm turns into astrologymania!

CAPRICORN

> You know what you have to do to get ahead. Take action now while you have the opportunity to make a difference. Show your fun side to superiors at work. Just be yourself. You have much to be thankful for and will gain praise and recognition if you are persistent. Share your ideas and be willing to take a chance. Don't let anyone tell you you cannot do something when you know you are fully capable.

This is Anne Marie's horoscope for the day. And regardless of whether you believe in signs, tarot cards, or the Easter Bunny, you'd have to concede that the words of her astrological forecast fit her in an uncanny way. Dear Annie does know what she needs to do to get ahead. And she is doing it, right here, right now. Taking action by learning to read. And the knit Marge Simpson hat, the jumbo soft drink, the Grand Canyon–wide smile, the concession stand in her backpack are all evidence of her fun side.

One more coincidence. That day at work it turns out Anne Marie courageously approached the housekeeping department's supervisor at the end of her shift with a suggestion. A few years back, due to budget reallocations, management stopped placing tiny chocolate kisses on the pillows in their guests' rooms. Anne Marie strongly thought the idea should be brought back to promote sweet dreams. Her supervisor loved it and even more loved Anne Marie, in his words, "sharing her ideas and taking a chance." He promised to bring it up at the next managers' meeting but was confident chocolate and pillows would soon be a couple once again.

We spend the first forty-five minutes of class breaking up the words. I can almost watch their minds operate as they apply all the things we've learned together.

For example, when we come to the word OPPORTUNITY, the class executes it like a Dale Earnhardt pit crew. First comes the opening sound, "O," like when you visit the doctor's office and you're asked to "open wide and say . . ." Next, they find small words inside the word itself. OR and IT. What sound does "Y" make at the end of a word? "E" like in EVE. How do we live our lives and love our loves? Answer: with Power. Harold completes the puzzle by noticing that TUN looks a whole lot like the word TUNE.

O PP OR TUN(e) IT E

Now comes the best part. I begin writing the words of another horoscope. This time for birthdays falling between

July 23 and August 22. Leos. Coincidentally, this happens to be Anne Marie's father's sign.

She says her pop, Jerome, is like a lion. "My daddy protects his family and gives us everything." Well, tonight his daughter is going to give him a big surprise.

LEO

> You come from strong stock and know how to dance with circumstances. Your common sense and clever wit entertain those around you, even as you prefer to hide them. Add time to your schedule for the unexpected. Sometimes you just have to pray and hope for the best. Sometimes it takes action and effort, despite the circumstances. Balance both.

You can't make this stuff up!

Sometimes accidents happen on purpose. And the contents of today's Leo horoscope would provide immeasurable blessings for this caring parent and his adult child. Letter by letter, sound by sound, word by word, the class takes apart Jerome's horoscope, and with each syllable Anne Marie's smile grows wider and wider.

"Oh my Lord, my daddy is strong as an ox. He works at a furniture store moving couches and chairs and tables all day long. He's been there for over forty years. And can he dance. Every Sunday you can't get him to sit down in church, and once he does, he's sweating so much his shirt sticks to his back."

Turns out today's astrological forecast has been written specifically with Papa Lion in mind on another point as well.

"Lord above, you gotta be kidding. Daddy tells a joke like nobody else. He starts laughing before he even gets the good part out."

My favorite portion of Leo's forecast, however, is the part about the "unexpected." Because tonight after dinner when dad and daughter excuse themselves from the table and move to the living room, Jerome is in store for an electrifying dessert. The whole shebang: whipped cream, chocolate sauce, nuts, and the cherry on top . . . His lion cub is going to read his fortune to him.

CHAPTER 24

Charles looks like a man of means, which makes the fact he spent a number of years as a homeless person almost impossible to conceive. But it's true. He has a past that Hollywood screenplays are modeled after. His childhood was poor at best—not only financially speaking, but emotionally. He left home at fifteen and hasn't seen any relatives in nearly forty years. He does, however, consider one person his family.

In 1991, Charles was living on the streets of Chicago in his cardboard studio under the Wacker Drive bridge. One July night he was shot. As the paramedics loaded him into the ambulance, a man handed Charles his business card. It turned out the stranger was a lawyer. But instead of trying to stir up litigation, the attorney's motives were quite the opposite. After getting out of the county hospital, Charles went directly to the address on the card. At their meeting, the lawyer told Charles he knew he was in a bad place because he himself had once been there. He also knew Charles was a heavy drug user. He paid for Charles to go to rehab and told him to contact him when he finished. Charles was at the rehab center for ninety days. The day he was released he showed up in the attorney's waiting room. As he sat in the high-back leather chair browsing among all the law books perfectly lined up in the bookcase, Charles could not believe this successful man had once been homeless too.

From that day forward, Charles never spent another night on the street. He began sleeping at the office and became the lawyer's personal bodyguard. In case I forgot to mention it, Charles is an intimidating figure. For the next eight years, Charles was gainfully employed as the attorney's protector, driver, and, ultimately, friend. On several occasions, he even appeared before judges to get continuances and file routine motions. According to Charles, the lawyer is the closest thing he's ever had to family. Even as his mentor now enjoys his retirement in Las Vegas, they remain close friends. The best part of the story is that Charles and his guardian angel wore the same size clothes. And shoes. And hats. Whenever the lawyer bought three new suits, his protégé would get three of his older ones. Charles suddenly looked like someone stepping right off page three in *GQ* magazine. To this day, he dresses like royalty. Prince Charles!

And fragrant? Every time I brush past him, I can't help being delighted by the scent of his cologne or aftershave. It reminds me of passing the perfume counter at the downtown department store where my mom took me shopping for school clothes at the end of each summer.

"Charles, you smell sensational. And if feeling that way is wrong, then I don't want to be right," I tease him. The corners of his mouth curl up, nearly reaching the lobes of his grand ears.

Even though he found his way off the streets, he still never learned to read. He memorized enough words to get by but wasn't able to master the task. Not for lack of trying, though. He now spends four or five days a week at the literacy center. Without hesitation, Charles is one of the most inspirational speakers I have ever heard. He speaks at each and every orientation Wednesday, detailing his story and emphasizing the theory behind hope. Only recently, after completing certain diagnostic testing, was it determined that despite having a well-above-average level of intelligence, he also suffers from a well-above-average learning disability that was never addressed. Guess who became my eighth student a few short weeks ago?

CHAPTER 25

As he gets closer and closer to the last page, the excitement around our house grows palpable. It is as if we are all monitoring the final landing of our great flying saucer as we return from an adventure in outer space. And in a way, we are. Because although Oliver is not about to settle on Mars or the Moon, he is indeed about to arrive in a solar system far beyond what he ever thought possible. Finishing *Black Beauty*. His very first book, cover to cover. The conquest that results in the accumulation of enough pennies to start his own mint.

Recently, he's relocated the growing fortune from the plastic plumber buckets to two of my aging, retired briefcases. I love that his achievement earnings found a new home inside cases that my own parents gave me as gifts, one on the night after I graduated from law school. And Oliver loves that they both have combination locks. He says it makes him feel like a spy.

Andi and I have made him promise that when he reaches the final page, he will stop and call us all in. So on that memorable Thursday evening on the twenty-third day of November at a little after eight thirty, he shouts from his room, "It's time, Mom and Dad. Bring Isabella and Sage!"

The four of us rush up those stairs as though it's feeding time at the fraternity house.

We all sit down on the floor with our legs crossed, waiting with the greatest anticipation. His biggest fans. Oliver stops at the very last sentence on page 281. He stands up from his bed, clears his throat, and with the poise, grace, and overacting of a seasoned soprano, serenades us with the story's last few words.

> My troubles are all over, and I am at home; and often before I am quite awake, I fancy I am still in the orchard at Birtwick, standing with my old friends under the apple trees.

As he finishes, he looks up at us with that Oliver smile. Pausing for grand finale effect, he raises his arms high in the air and yells, "THE END!"

In triumphant harmony, we all jump up and cheer. When the ovations finally simmer down, Oliver stands before Andi and me with tears of joy scaling down his ruby-flushed cheeks and whispers, "I did it, Mom and Dad. I did it." We take him in our arms and hold him like we never plan on letting him go until he leaves for college. As my wife's eyes and mine meet, we know our little astronaut is going to be all right.

Eventually we throw him back onto his bed. Then, along with Isabella and Sage, we tickle him as we repeat the last line of the book. "I'm Oliver and my troubles are all over and I am at home . . . with my old friends under the apple trees."

And at the end, Oliver reaches under his bed, pulls out one of his briefcases, and clicks it open. "Who wants ice cream? I'm buying!"

CHAPTER 26

Sometimes a coincidence is just that. An accident. A stroke of luck. A fluke of nature. So I guess what happens that Wednesday afternoon in early December has nothing to do with fate or some higher intervention. For me, however, it is a slice of spooky and gives me reason to speculate whether perhaps someone has bugged my little boy's bedroom. (For the record, let me clarify that at no time have I ever discussed with anyone at the literacy center what book Oliver has been reading and ultimately finished just thirteen days earlier.)

After spending several weeks writing, dissecting, and reading everyone's horoscopes, we are all astrologically forecasted out. It is time for a change. So I decide we are ready for something new, something a bit more challenging.

"How would you like to read a book together?"

"You mean *the book*?" asks Anne Marie as she grabs hold of the Bible from her sewing bag.

"No, no. Not that book." She frowns. "Not that *that* book wouldn't be fun to read," I stammer. "I mean, my God, we all need a little more of *that* book, right?" I glance over in Michael's direction.

"Amen to that," chimes in Gail. And then she and Anne Marie begin sparring back and forth with their favorite tales. The Lord's Creation of Earth. The Garden of Eden. Adam and Eve. Esther. The Nativity. Joseph and His Brothers. Babylon. Moses. Jonah. Daniel in the Lion's Den. It's like Scripture ping-pong. When one of them eventually volleys back Virgin Mary, Michael seizes the moment and jumps on board.

"F—in' Mary. Fraud. No such thing as a woman virgin. Immaculate conception, my a—."

Anne Marie hands Gail a tissue from her travel pack, and together they start fanning themselves.

I squeeze in and pray for Michael not to cause an irreverent uproar. Literally. "Michael, I'm begging you, please don't make Gail or Anne Marie violate the Sixth Commandment."

Surprisingly, he heeds my pleas and stops making any further sacrilegious statements. After the heat turns down and Michael tenders a Michael-like apology, we continue discussing our own next adventure of biblical proportions.

"So I was thinking we should choose a book that we all like and then we could read it together. Start our own kind of book club."

"Like Oprah," yells out Melvin.

"Yeah, like Oprah."

Michael gets a second wind. "Oprah motherf—"

"MICHAEL!" This time everyone laughs. Even our two church ladies.

The plan is for everyone to bring in a book the following week. Any book they want, just as long as it isn't too easy, à la Dr. Seuss's *Green Eggs and Ham*, or too hard, à la Tolstoy's *War and Peace*. Preferably, something exciting and something enjoyable for both men and women.

"So I guess *Playboy* is out of the question?" (Yes, that would be Michael.)

We would arrange all of the selections on my desk and vote on which one to read. I was almost positive none of my students had ever officially completed an entire book, so this undertaking would be quite an adventure. It would be a slow process but worth it. Just as the Fab Five had done in Miss Hughes's class with *My Life*, we'd pass the six-word "snowballs" around the circle. Everybody would get enough time on stage to make it challenging but not enough to ever make it deflating. Every unknown word would go up on the blackboard for dissection and dismemberment, ultimately to be mended together again. I was just hoping it wouldn't take us as long to read it as it took the author to write it.

The following Wednesday when I arrive at class, six books, one magazine, and one game/puzzle periodical are lined up on my desk. Melvin brings in a travel magazine with a picture of Denzel Washington on its cover that he "borrowed" from his podiatrist's office. Next to his magazine is Edna's selection: *SUDOKU: 100 Fun Number Brain Teasers*. Not only not great reading material, but I have never been able to complete more than two of those boxes.

Harold loves nothing more in this world than his birthplace, New Orleans, Louisiana. His face beams whenever he speaks of his childhood there: Mardi Gras. Ten thousand Cajun recipes his grandma knew by heart. Jazz 24/7. So it is no great surprise that his selection, *Chasing the Devil's Tail*, is a thriller about a Creole detective who systematically solves crimes in the streets of the Big Easy. Now this is something we can sink our teeth into.

But I quickly realize this wonderful piece of literature may not make the cut in our humble classroom. As I glance at the overview on the back cover, I find this glowing summary: "In the raucous, bloody, red-light district of Storyville, New Orleans, in 1907, where two thousand scarlet women practice their trade, where cocaine and opium are sold over the counter, and where rye whiskey flows like an amber river, there's a killer loose. Someone is murdering Storyville prostitutes and marking each killing with a black rose." Perhaps next semester.

Five books remain. Ever since Charles joined our group, it was easy to see he was a football fanatic. He could spend hours and hours arguing about who was the greatest running back ever. It always came down to three: Jim Brown, Walter Payton, and Gayle Sayers. So of course when I see *I Am Third*, the story about the friendship between Gayle Sayers and Brian Piccolo, I immediately know whose selection it is.

A neighbor had given Gail one of John Grisham's first books, *A Pelican Brief*, which coincidentally also starred Denzel Washington. Gail had read the first few pages at home and thought maybe this would be a good fit for the class.

All unique and interesting selections, but that's not where fate crosses my desk. It is the remaining three that send goose pimples across my back.

Anne Marie has worked overtime at the hotel and forgets to bring in a book. That is all right, though, because her friend Elvira brings in two. Over the weekend, she has been shopping at the flea market on 95th Street near her house when she comes to a table selling old books. For fifty cents, she buys two with the same title: one for her and one for Anne Marie. Inside on the dedication page Elvira writes, "To my friend, Annie. Baby Steps. Vera." The title on those two copies is *Black Beauty*. When Elvira gives it to her, Anne Marie begins to cry. In between the tears, we learn what sets off her emotion.

"I have had this book in my bedroom for a long, long time. Since I was a little girl. Every time I picked it up and tried to read it, I couldn't. It's all dented from me throwing it against the wall."

Turns out Elvira has absolutely no idea this particular book means so much to her friend. The two have never discussed it before. Aren't coincidences grand?

The last book resting on my desk is Michael's selection. As I look down to see just what it could possibly be, those goose pimples turn into goose boulders. Because on the front cover of Michael's book are the words *Black Beauty*. Before you ask, Michael has never met my son Oliver, and when he's not launching F-bombs around the room, he barely speaks to either Anne Marie or Elvira. So I have to ask.

"Michael, how did you choose that book?"

With the thumb and first finger sticking out from the top of his leather glove, he caresses the goatee encircling his upper lip, mouth, and chin. After an uncomfortably long pause—surely premeditated for effect—he speaks.

"What else would I pick? This book perfectly describes me. I'm black and I'm a beauty!"

That night I go to Barnes & Noble and purchase five more copies. We now have our own bible. Unfortunately, I never make it to the first page.

CHAPTER 27

Ever since he could talk, Oliver and I have played the Cloud Game. He was a pro right from the start. "There's Barney wearing cowboy boots. There's Barney wearing a cowboy hat. There's Barney dancing with a bear." Although I never truly saw Barney, that purple dinosaur sure got a lot of play up in Oliver's wild blue yonder. I played the same game with my mom when I was a little boy. I remember standing with her in the backyard of our duplex gazing at the sky and trying to find the one-legged giraffe from my picture book or the caterpillar with an earring hanging from its nose that was my favorite character from the project my mom and I cowrote when I was in the third grade.

She was never not there for me. I hope I make it in time.

As the jet climbs higher and higher, I stare out the window, and through my tears, I can see shadows of the different puffy pillows of grays and whites resting in various areas of the dark blue water of Lake Michigan. Each suddenly transforms itself into something other than just a simple condensed vapor of water or ice: A turtle wearing a turban. Richard Nixon blowing smoke out of his mouth. A crime-fighting woodpecker with a giant fist soaring through the sky.

As I continue looking out the window, the turban-topped turtle and the superhero woodpecker quickly disappear. As if they had never been there. Which is exactly what I wonder, later, as I walk into the Critical Care Unit of the Delray Beach Medical Center. Is this really my mom or simply a shadow of her old self? I can't believe it's her lying on her back in this room that smells of baby powder. We saw each other just a few short weeks ago. The woman who gave me life is now turning in the direction of death? Her face has tripled in size as a result of all the medication. She wears plastic glasses purchased from the checkout counter at Walgreens because she's unable to put in her contact lenses any longer due to the blood clot in her right eye.

I hate her. Sixty-nine years old and she's giving in. She's too young to die and I'm too young to be a motherless child. I think everyone should mourn someone they love before it's too late. During life. It's important to be sad about losing something while it's still here.

In layman's terms, my mom has an infection in her blood that is creating chemicals that are eating away at her insides.

As she lies here helpless and alone, I want to cry. Not just for her, but for time. How fast life is going.

Only yesterday, it seems, I remember this same scent of powder filling the hallways in our house. With twins, Andi and I were constantly changing diapers. I loved pouring powder on their scrumptious bitty behinds. When I'd have to leave for work, I intentionally forgot to wash the powder off my hands so that when I was miles away from home, I could raise my palms to my nose and the twins would still be with me. But now that smell is gone. Forever. I find myself so afraid of passing time I try not paying attention to it. I even stopped wearing a watch. Last year, the clock in my car burned out. I still haven't replaced the bulb.

Liza, the Filipino nurse, finishes sponge bathing my mom and now begins changing her sheets.

"Do you need some help?" I ask.

"Sure, of course I do, sweetie," she says with a soothing smile. As she rolls my mom onto her side, I place one hand on my mother's back and the other as a support for her left shoulder. Her body is so warm. I can feel the heat through my wedding ring. Mom moans in pain as the nurse removes the sheet from beneath her brittle and bruised skin.

"Breathe, Mom, breathe," I say.

"It hurts so bad, Robbie," she cries. (She's the only person in the world I still let call me by that nickname.)

"Call me Jimmie, Mom. You know how I'm still angry you and Dad didn't name me . . . Jimmmmie!" I enunciate in a slow, exaggerated drawl. We all laugh together.

I turn and stare out the window, my eyes glued to the ocean and all the high-rise condominiums surrounding it. I count each of their floors like they're sheep, wishing this was all just a dream. But it's not. One of the buildings reminds me of the place where I rented my very first apartment when I left home. I thought that was the beginning of my adulthood. It turns out every day is the beginning of adulthood. Starting your own business. Getting married. Buying a home. Having babies. And today, helping change the sheets in your mom's hospital room as she lies in pain, grasping for life.

I continue whispering for her to breathe so she can relax, all the while watching a complete stranger wearing white working in dignified silence. I'm not sure if it's the baby powder or the sunlight coming through the window, but as I stare down at my mom's shoulder, her skin looks so young. And pure. The freckles on her back resemble those on a little girl. And as we make eye contact, there's a sense of peace for both of us. Without saying a word, we tell each other that this, too, is okay and is simply just another beginning of adulthood.

CHAPTER 28

As a dad, you try to make as many personal appearances at your children's activities as possible. Therefore, over the years you will find yourself, like me, trampling upon a variety of different traffic violations cataloged in the Illinois Vehicle Code. Whether it's speeding to a ballet recital held in the basement of the local church for your fourteen-month-old pretty-in-pink daughter or driving on the shoulder of the road for better than a mile to make it in time for your son's third-grade talent show, you'll do just about anything to be there. Nothing can keep you away. Except, of course, when your own mother is dying.

Consequently, when Oliver's prize for finishing his first book is ready, I am not there for the big day. He calls me from the back room at Toys 'R' Us where Ernesto and Gary have meticulously assembled his motorized all-terrain vehicle.

"Dad, you can't believe this thing. It's freaking beautifuuuuuullll. It's got everything. The two different speeds . . . the towing hook in the back . . . it looks just like a real ATV. Oh, and the radio does work." It does. He holds the phone down so I can listen to the static. "See, I told you it was real!"

"You were right, Big Man. And you should be proud of yourself. You did it. I'm sorry I'm not there so you can give me a ride. Was the person at the cash register mad?"

I had made Andi promise me that Oliver would pay for his new wheels with the money he earned from reading. The store manager came out to the parking lot to help our son carry in his bulky briefcases from the car. All thirty-six thousand pennies! Andi paid the $34.20 in tax with paper money and two dimes. Rather than count it all out and create a traffic jam, after hearing his story and seeing the stern and credible expression on Oliver's face, the cashier simply emptied the copper contents of the cases into an extra strength Hefty bag and had Gary—the same one who helped assemble the ATV—drag it away.

"Okay, Big Man, I have to go now. Tell Mommy I love her and give Belly and Sage a kiss from me."

"Hey Daddy, I miss you. When you coming home? How's Grammy?"

"I'll be home soon. Grammy is getting better."

I wouldn't. And she wasn't. As I hang up the phone, I close my eyes and picture Oliver roaring down our back alley as he takes the inaugural flight on his new blazing orange ATV.

His teeth shining bright, his golden brown hair flowing in the wind, his radio blaring. It must have been just the same for *Black Beauty* as he ran free for the first time.

CHAPTER 29

"What was the last word you said to your mommy in the hospital before she died?" asks six-year-old Sage.

As I clutch onto the phone receiver listening to Sage's beating breath as he waits for a response to his grown-up question, I can feel the tears dripping down my wrist. I keep hearing the words my mom would say every time we'd argue over something silly like cleaning my room or breaking curfew. "You only get one mom." She was right. And now, I no longer have one. But my youngest son is waiting for an answer. So I tell him the story, unlike any other bedtime tale he's heard.

As my two brothers and I sit together in Room 905 of the intensive care unit on that Sunday night, frosty reality begins to set in. Hope quickly turns into fate, which seems only moments away from sorrow. I have memorized all the relevant numbers and their respective meanings on the screens of the multiple machines hooked up to her body. Mom looks like a science project. But as long as that one bottom number stays above sixty, we have a chance.

Somewhere between hope and fate comes negotiation. Three grown men sit bargaining with God, discussing which terms we can accept and which ones we cannot. As if we have a choice in the matter. Our dad can't bear the conversation and waits outside.

A few minutes later, her doctor joins us. "I'm sorry about your mom. Can we go and talk for a moment?"

In single-file fashion, we march out and follow him into the hallway.

"Things have unfortunately taken a turn for the worse," he begins. "Your mom's blood pressure is at thirty-five. Any chance of recovery at this point is highly improbable."

Silence. Improbable is defined as having a probability too low to inspire belief. Our mom always inspired her three boys to believe in anything. Santa Claus, the Tooth Fairy, and the guarantee that moms live forever. She was the one who convinced me to take the law school entrance exam.

"Has anyone discussed with you the DNR?" he asks.

Do not resuscitate.

Standing in the presence of strangers, we are now being asked to give up on the woman who gave us life.

After signing the document, we return to Room 905 and sit together on the edge of the air-conditioner unit, each getting his opportunity to say something private and personal and eternal to the person we have known longest on this planet. When it's my turn, I put my nose on her cold cheek. I can barely hear her breathing. Her chest quietly moves up and down.

The last word I said to my mommy, I tell Sage, was the word son. "I loved being your son."

CHAPTER 30

Andi, Isabella, Oliver, and Sage arrive at Miami International Airport a little after midnight. We stay up until after four sharing stories about my mom. After sleeping an hour or so, I get up to shower and get ready for a day you never plan to get ready for.

Every morning at home, my daughter and I go through the same ritual. We've been doing it since she was six or seven. She picks out the perfect tie for me to wear to work—the one she thinks goes best with my suit and my eyes. She always wants her daddy to look just right.

Today, however, I want to look especially nice. Andi and Isabella bring me a few to choose from. As I stand alone inside the closet of my parents' guest room in the dark, I see Isabella waiting just beyond the door. I wonder how long she's been there. Everyone else is still asleep. I can barely hear her breathing. She's trying not to disturb me.

"Hey Belly," I say. As if there's some electronic force field preventing her from entering, she won't cross the seam in the carpet dividing the bedroom area from the entry of the closet. "You want to help me pick out my tie? I'm having a tough time with this one."

She remains silent and shakes her head back and forth. I can't believe how much she looks like Andi. "You look beautiful, princess girl. Go put on your shoes and let's get everyone up. We can't be late."

She cautiously crosses the barrier and slowly approaches me. She stops an inch or two away. Her cheek rests on the black torn ribbon the rabbi gave us last night and which I've pinned to my shirt. I'll wear this badge on my chest for the next thirty days as a sign of respect in the grief process. She gently tilts her head upward and looks me dead center in my eyes. She wraps her arms around me and squeezes like she's just learned that the hiding place of the bogeyman really is under her bed. After a few seconds, she lets go, turns around, and walks out. Not a word was spoken between us, but I know exactly what my sweet girl is saying. "I'm sorry you are about to put your mommy in the ground."

Of all the words and thoughts and sentiments I receive during the mourning of my loss, the silence spoken by my favorite daughter on the morning of my mom's funeral is by far the most comforting. It helps me pick out the perfect tie—the one with all the smiley faces.

CHAPTER 31

On the final day of the mourning period, my dad and my brothers and I end shivah week by taking a short ritualistic walk together around the block. We all hold hands, which I can't remember ever doing before. As we turn the corner and head back toward the finish line where all the spouses, children, and other onlookers wait, my dad decides it is the perfect time to share some important news with us.

"Dr. Mandell thinks I should have the surgery this Wednesday." "This Wednesday" is in two days. The surgery he is speaking of is double heart-valve replacement, a procedure he has been dodging for nearly seven years. A procedure five different cardiologists have been recommending for these same eighty-four months. For some reason, however, "this Wednesday" at long last seems like the opportune time to heed their advice.

My dad always knew best. About surgeries to have. Movies to see. Girlfriends to not see. Business . . . cheeses . . . and even roadways. When I arrived from Chicago a few days ago, I was twenty minutes late. "Did you take I-95?" he asked. "No, I took the 101." "See!"

Ironically, my mom had spent the last several years trying to convince her husband to preserve his life, and she was the one who ended up dying.

Being the eldest son means many things. As a teenager, you get to sit in the front seat on Sunday morning drives to the flea market with your dad and two younger brothers searching through other people's junk for treasures. You are also the first one called up to the podium by the rabbi to speak at your mother's funeral service. And as senior sibling, you will be the one who volunteers to stay back in steamy Florida to supervise the patient during his six-week recuperation after heart surgery. Somehow riding shotgun all those Sundays no longer seems so majestic.

So the next morning we pack up the rental van with everyone's belongings except mine and I drive the four centers of my world to the airport. As we stand together near the security line pretending six weeks is only a month and fourteen days, our bodies are linked like we were conjoined at birth.

Oliver takes me by the hand and walks me away from the others. When we are far enough away so nobody else can hear, he lets go of my hand and looks up into my eyes. Through his tears, he says, "Don't worry, Dad, I will take care of them while you're gone. And I'll try to not be so mean to Isabella."

Now we are both crying. "I know that, Big Man. Why do you think I call you 'Big Man'?"

And then his next words nearly knock me to the floor. Something I never expected from him. Something I could never have predicted.

"Dad. I know you got a lot of worries in your head. You got us, work, and your reading class. I can't help you with work. But I can help with the other two."

Where was he going with this?

"Besides being the man of the house while you're taking care of Poppi, I can also teach your class when you're gone. I know what it feels like to feel stupid and not know how to read. I can do it. I think they'll really like me."

They will love him. But not more than I do.

CHAPTER 32

"Robbie. Robbie, you up? Wake up, Robbie. Now. I need to tell you something," my dad whispers as he jerks my left shoulder up and down. I reluctantly open my eyes, and in the dark I find my dad sitting next to me on the edge of the bed wearing a white undershirt with matching white bikini briefs that fit him better fifty pounds ago. And one black dress sock. There are spaghetti sauce stains running up and down near the neckline of the undershirt.

"What is it, Dad? What's wrong?"

"I can't do it, Son. I just can't."

At first, I think he may be referring to going on without my mom. The idea of living without her is too much for him to bear. But that isn't it. What he can't do is his surgery. A surgery that is scheduled to take place in exactly five hours and twenty-six minutes.

"You're just going to have to call them up and tell them we changed our mind," he instructed.

In the past, I have been sympathetic to my dad's apprehension. Mindful of his fear of going under the knife. But not this time. Not with five hours and twenty-six minutes to go. Not after I have just sent my own quartet back to Chicago without me. And not after I just lost my mom. At last count, I only have one parent left. I'm not about to let his stubbornness make me a full-fledged orphan.

The surgery takes nearly seven hours. Dad spends sixteen days in the ICU afterward, but the procedure is a success.

During that time, I read two novels, miserably try to learn how to play Sudoku, and eat an incomprehensible amount of junk food out of hospital vending machines. Most of all, I spend my time missing my wife and our three kids. Nights are the worst. As a man, you think you'll yearn for some alone time. Until you have it. And then you realize just how lonely alone can feel.

On my eighth day away, Oliver calls me at eleven forty-five at night. I can tell he is calling from our basement because the connection from down there always makes it sound like you're phoning from inside a submarine.

"Hey, Big Man, why are you still up? And what are you doing in the basement?" I ask.

"Because I want to talk to you in private," he echoes.

"What's up, Big O?"

"Well, I've been thinking a lot about our talk at the airport. Who *is* gonna teach your people while you are away?"

Earlier in the week, I had spoken with Aunt June Porter and explained the situation about my dad and his surgery. She already knew about my mom. In fact, three days after the funeral I got a UPS delivery filled with sympathy cards from all my students. In respect for my loss, Michael wrote five whole words without using one single F-bomb. A personal record. Harold and Anne Marie sent copies of various scripture verses and psalms specifically geared to comfort me during my time of grief. They created a homemade scrapbook, bound with a yellow ribbon, filled with pictures of our class waving and throwing kisses. In the care package was a sweet note from Gail with a copy of her mama's secret pecan pie recipe that nobody else outside the family had ever been privy to. At the bottom she wrote, "The key is to add the extra 2½ teaspoons of vanilla. Shhhh! If you have any questions, call me after seven thirty at night. God bless you and your family."

Oliver continues. I can tell by the pace of his speech that he has rehearsed the subject a great deal. "I was thinking a lot about your class and how it's not fair they have to stop reading just because you're not there. What if I just stopped reading? I'd never have finished *Black Beauty* and I'd never have gotten my ATV."

I was touched by his earlier offer as we bid farewell at the airport, but I never thought any more about it because I knew it wasn't in the realm of possibility.

"So what are you saying, Oliver? What do you want me to do?" As I wait for his answer, I notice my mom's bathrobe hanging on the hook on the back of the bathroom door.

"I can do it," he announces.

"What?" I say. "Do what, Oliver?"

"I can teach them," he declares confidently, with a capital C. "I'll be your substitute teacher."

Fathers surprise sons with presents and sons surprise fathers with gifts. I start crying. Except for the first time in weeks, my tears are being shed because of happiness, not sorrow. As a dad, you wonder if your kids are ever really buying what you're selling. I now knew my eldest son had heard me.

Sounds crazy, right? A twelve-year-old holding court in a room full of adult illiterates helping them read. And not just any twelve-year-old. A boy with a learning disability who up until a very short time ago couldn't sound out the letter B. But nothing in my life over the last several weeks had seemed "normal."

"Okay, Big Man, let me sleep on it, all right? Yes, I promise, I'll think about it. Yes, I'll call you in the morning before school. I know, I know. You really are a good reader now. Tell everybody I love them. Nite, sweet dreams. Love you more."

CHAPTER 33

I wish I could tell you that my class liked Oliver as much as they liked me. I can't. They liked him more. Over time, I had spoken so much about this boy they felt they already knew him, even though they had never met. It hadn't been hard convincing Aunt June Porter to go along with the idea. She quickly saw the poetic justice of the situation. All she required was the class's approval, a signed authorization by Andi and me, and Oliver's completion of the tutor's seminar. She agreed to personally lead the accelerated program, which she condensed and customized specifically for a younger person. Twin sister joined him, and together the pair became the youngest persons ever to be certified as reading tutors at Literacy Chicago's center. They stopped off at the Dollar Store near our house to buy frames for their certificates.

My phone rings and I hear two voices howling into the receiver at the same time. Even though they are different genders, they are still young enough to make it nearly impossible for me to tell them apart. Belly and Oliver frequently take advantage of this fact.

"Calm down, calm down," I say. They can't. They are both so excited about the day's events, they felt like they'd been to Disneyland. They tell me about the band of street performers sitting on milk crates playing their white buckets under the streetlights. I hear all about Preacher Man and everything he opposes.

"Daddy," Isabella asks, "why do so many things send you to hell? Does that mean Uncle Stu is going to hell?" (Stuart is everybody's favorite uncle who just happens to be gay.)

Isabella and Oliver loved the old elevator that carried them up to the literacy center, which now had its very own operator. Pete wears a Philadelphia Phillies baseball cap and is missing a thumb on his right hand. For some reason, Oliver found that to be the coolest part of the whole day.

Isabella and Oliver's first session goes off without a hitch. Oliver is a born teacher. Perhaps the old saying "those who can't do, teach" should be modified to "those who couldn't, but now can, do." And after his and Belly's second session with the GEMS, I receive a cute text from Aunt June Porter telling me to feel free to stay in the Sunshine State as long as necessary. Apparently, not only are the students receptive to Isabella and Oliver, they can't get enough of my offspring. Sometimes adults who can't read relate better to children than to grown-ups because little people are much less judgmental.

(Andi has two severely mentally handicapped cousins, so early on our twins were introduced to the concept that not everybody is identical.) More important, Oliver is one of them, and they know he gets it.

Belly loves music. All kinds of music. And dancing. She started taking dance lessons when she was three, and by five she was performing in competitions. I remember the amazement that filled the ballroom during her ballet performance just before her tenth birthday. She had chosen "You Can't Always Get What You Want" by the Rolling Stones for her audition. She wore glittery Converse high-tops and a yellow tank top with the band's trademark swollen red lips stenciled in the center while every other girl on stage was pirouetting to *The Nutcracker* and *Swan Lake*.

So it's no great surprise when I hear that Isabella's teaching session involves songs.

"Please put away your copies of *Black Beauty*," she politely asked the eight aging faces looking up at her and her brother from their seats. "We are going to try something different today."

An hour before any of their students arrived, Oliver and Isabella had used both the whiteboard and the blackboard in the room to write out the words of their personal favorite songs. Belly's, of course, was the hit released by the Stones in 1969. Early on in our journey as parents, we introduced them to Mick and his mates, and Isabella became an instant fan.

At the top of Oliver's billboard chart was "The Green Grass Grew All Around," the nursery song with ten cumulative verses I sang endlessly to Oliver during the first four and a half years of his life to help him fall asleep.

After Isabella explained why their favorite songs were written on the board, she asked everyone else in the room to name theirs. Some called out titles instantly; others had to give it some thought. By the end, they had composed their class album—a sheet of yellow paper filled with eight songs consisting of some of the zaniest titles you ever heard. The idea was brilliant: My dynamic substitute teachers would print out the lyrics, make copies for each student, and buy the songs from iTunes to be played at a jam session on Isabella's iPod after each song was successfully read. Einstein-like!

Gail started the party off with an oldie but goodie!

Amazing grace, how sweet the sound,
That saved a wretch like me.
I once was lost but now am found,
Was blind, but now I see.
'Twas grace that taught
my heart to fear.
And grace my fears relieved.
How precious did that grace appear
the hour I first believed.
Through many dangers, toils, and snares
we have already come.
'Twas grace that brought us safe thus far
and grace will lead us home.
The Lord has promised good to me.
His word my hope secures.
He will my shield and portion be
as long as life endures.
When we've been there ten thousand years
bright shining as the sun.
We've no less days to sing God's praise
than when we first begun.
Amazing grace, how sweet the sound,
That saved a wretch like me.
I once was lost but now am found,
Was blind, but now I see.

After six verses packed with eye-opening inspiration, the room itched for more.

Harold was up next with "Down Home Blues" by ZZ Hill and George Jackson. They all chipped in dissecting phraseologies like kicking off your shoes . . . party down . . . on the town . . . and keeping cool.

In a matter of moments, Isabella and Oliver had magically transported sweet ole Harold back to St. Peter Street in the French Quarter of his motherland. After everyone else had left the room and Isabella was gathering her belongings to go home, she said she could still hear Harold humming the song to himself as he erased the lyrics from the blackboard.

CHAPTER 34

During the previous few months, I sometimes heard Anne Marie or Edna speaking under their breath whenever Michael artfully hurled out another of his profane verbal gems. They'd mumble things like, "Doing the devil's work for him" or, "Do not allow Satan to whisper in your ear" in response to one of his unedited earfuls. One day when he chucked something obscene about somebody's mama, classically reserved Edna came a tad undone. Literally. The top button of her sweater popped off from the internal explosion as she shrieked like a kitten getting its tail run over by a moving vacuum cleaner. "Listen to John, my brother. Listen to John."

"Who the f— is John?" Michael inquired.

At the time, I had no idea who she was talking about either. We never had a John in our class, and I didn't recall that name ever being mentioned before. Nevertheless, I was curious, so I looked it up on the computer when I got home. In the New Testament book of John, chapter 2, verses 10 and 11, the disciple of Jesus talks about the ills of gossiping and how people should bite their tongue before they go around blathering about someone else's dirty laundry. And not only should you refrain from gossiping, you also should forever keep from even listening to the mere tinkling of a gossiping tongue.

It is no great shock, therefore, when Isabella asks me if I ever heard of the Williams Brothers (I hadn't) and tells me about Anne Marie's song selection: "Sweep Around Your Own Front Door." In other words, mind your own beeswax and take a vacation from slinging arrows at your neighbor.

The gospel song gives new meaning to the Golden Rule, and the stanza that speaks of replacing the hate in your heart with love is especially powerful.

As the song came to an end, Oliver said it was the first time since he met him that Michael's mouth was out of bullets. He sat speechless, tightly gripping the arms of his wheelchair and searching for something, anything to say. When he finally did decide to open his mouth, the class quickly convinced him to close it. Together, like they had rehearsed it for a middle school play, they all individually stacked their fists one on top of the other and began moving their make-believe brooms back and forth, miming as a group the act of sweeping Michael's illicit thoughts into fairy dust. Boy, I wish I had been there to see that!

CHAPTER 35

When Isabella and Oliver called that night to tell me about their class's rock fest, I wasn't home because there had been an emergency at the hospital. The nurses had changed my dad's pain medication and he was having a negative reaction. I could hear the screams of agony the moment I stepped off the elevator. After we finally calmed him down and he fell back asleep, I myself was exhausted and decided it was safe for me to head back to my parents' home to get some shut-eye.

As I got into the car, I reached for my cell phone, which I had left on the front seat, started the engine, and began listening to my voicemail. Once again a Higher Being was watching over me because the recorded message was more like a thirty-minute infomercial, and the phone captured every single word and note of it!

At first, I couldn't hear a thing because two voices were simultaneously yelling into the receiver. Eventually I figured out they were negotiating who would get to play which song. After a brief pause, the concert began.

Even white guys who can't dance couldn't help but move to the music that was playing through my headset. I felt the power from it in my bones. I was shaking and shimmying all the way down Interstate 95, and as I pulled up to pay the two dollars and fifty cents, the tollbooth operator wondered whether she should call the local authorities. I didn't care, though. I needed to dance, and dance I did. Right there inside that rented dirty Chevy van.

After listening to Gail's "Amazing Grace," Harold's "Down Home Blues," and Anne Marie's "Sweep Around Your Own Front Door," next came Melvin's "Cooling Water," coincidentally also by the Williams Brothers. All about a person's soul being overcome by the sins of the world, but the love of God, through Jesus, rescuing that soul.

Ironically, I would never associate Melvin with any part of a world of sin. Perhaps his selection had more to do with the wife who abandoned his daughter and him.

The hits kept coming:

Edna: "Turn Back the Hands" by Tyrone Davis.

Elvira: "Love and Happiness" by Al Green.

Charles: "Every Day I Have the Blues" by Count Basie and His Orchestra.

And Michael? Dolly Parton's "I Will Always Love You" sung by Whitney Houston!

You can't imagine how it felt flying down that empty Florida turnpike at one thirty in the morning with all six windows rolled down and listening to those incredible horn sections blaring from Isabella's iPod.

When the music finally disappeared, Oliver grabbed the phone and started detailing their day. He was so excited I could almost hear the drip of the little drops of saliva he gets in between the gaps of his teeth whenever he tells a story too fast. I could also hear Isabella pulling for the phone in the background.

He explained how they wrote each song on the board and how every person took a turn calling out a specific word whenever he or Isabella pointed to it. How they knew most of the words because a lot of them were ones they'd already memorized from the Dolch list. And the ones they didn't know, they broke up together "just like we do, Dad."

"But the best part, Dad," Oliver concluded his description. "The best part is after we finished reading the whole song, Isabella played it on her iPod. And then they all got up and started dancing. Even Michael. Well, he didn't get up, but you know what I mean."

Oliver took a gulp of air before he finished. "I swear to God, Dad. Everybody. The whole room was crazy. Anne Marie was shaking her butt so hard I thought it was going to fall off. And then Mrs. Aunt June Porter came running in to see what was going on, and you can't believe her face. She was like, 'Oh my Lord.' At first I thought she was going to be mad at us. But then she started laughing. It was like the part in that movie *Blues Brothers* we watched where they're all dancing in the church doing flips and everything. It was crazy, Dad. *Crazy*. I wish you were there."

I just had been.

CHAPTER 36

As a child, I was raised in a no-color zone. So even before we had kids, Andi and I always planned on raising our family in the Big City. Skyscrapers, traffic jams, and many different shades. Half of Isabella and Oliver's class at Lakeshore Preparatory preschool was African American. From their first day of finger-painting class, our twins were color-blind.

I had warned (admonished) them about Michael before they began serving as my substitute teachers. "Think of his F's like they're mosquitoes," I said. "They're annoying, but they can't hurt you." The first time they officially met, Michael was verbally restrained and even took off his leather glove before he shook Isabella's hand. When I learned about that introduction, I knew they were safe.

Most tutors never even know the last names of their students, let alone ever choose to socialize with them. But my connection with the GEMS had turned into something much greater than most of the other relationships. Our situation wasn't planned; it just evolved. Just like that night we all went out to celebrate. The night Michael and I broke the boundary line between us. The night I probably owe Aunt June and the center an apology for.

It was the last class before break. Somebody suggested we go across the street to Clive's, a small bar that had been in the neighborhood for forty-plus years and apparently the only chunk of real estate not gobbled up by Bennigans, Benetton, Baby Gap, and Borders. It was a little after six, so I thought what could one drink and a plate of chicken wings hurt? Charles and Harold each had a beer, and Edna surprisingly nursed a generous glass of scotch. Michael ordered a vodka, so I felt obliged to do the same. We all sat around a big old wooden table surrounded by pistachio shells.

I couldn't help noticing how giggly and glassy-eyed Edna had suddenly turned even though her glass was still half full of Johnnie Walker Red Label. She looked like a New Year's Eve partygoer. Everyone listened intently as I shared how Anna Sewell wrote *Black Beauty* in the last years of her life, while confined to her house as an invalid. And how she died only five months after the book was published, so she never knew how popular—and lucrative—it had become.

Slowly the group started to dwindle. Soon it was just Michael and me sitting with the abandoned bottles of beer and glasses of soda pop on the tabletop.

By eight forty-five, we had polished off two more drinks apiece. The last round was on the house after we beat a pair of regulars in a game of darts. In those two hours together, I discovered a life span about my new friend. A friendship that would remain classified once we left that bar.

He learned to read very early on and, according to him, was finishing grown-up books by seven. But then his AWOL dad returned to the family home and began beating him.

"Just like Cheerios, my daddy had at me every morning," he said. "Sometimes so bad I couldn't even sit at my desk in school. I'd have to do something to get the teacher to send me to the principal's office."

As a result, he eventually climbed inside himself, shut off the lights, and gave up on everything, including his studies. "My daddy's knuckles beat the smarts right out of me." I glanced down at his leather gloves. "I became just another black kid [he didn't use the word *black*] walking the streets."

By the time we left the bar, we were both well over the legal limit. I flagged down a cab. When it pulled up, I stood there motionless, gazing into the moonlit sky wondering about my next move. The cab stood higher than your traditional four-door taxi. It was a minivan and its seats were elevated. Michael couldn't lift himself up into it. He looked at my vodka-infused eyes waiting for me to call the next play. So, like a rookie quarterback in for the first time, I did. I reached under his armpits and pulled him out of the wheelchair and into the air. He was remarkably light, and I held him in front of me for a second or two like a trusting toy soldier. It was awkwardly comfortable. As I bent over and eased his reduced body into the cab, I could feel his dependence through my pistachio-red-stained fingers. He maneuvered himself the rest of the way across the backseat. I climbed in beside him and closed the door. We never spoke about that event again and each sat looking straight out into the dark.

When we arrived in front of his apartment building, the taxi driver got the wheelchair out from the back and held it open while Michael slid off into it. I said good-bye and watched him wheel away while the building's security guard held the front door open. I could almost hear Michael's response of "None of your f—in' business" after the aging guard inquired, "How was your night?" I laughed out loud but didn't explain my private joke to the cabbie.

As we got back on the highway I shut my eyes, pretending I was blind, and didn't open them until we got to the front of my house.

CHAPTER 37

"Aren't you shocked, Daddy, that he picked the "I Will Always Love You" song?" asks Isabella.

I'm not. It makes perfect sense. Of course, afterward, everyone teases him, and Michael quickly defends his selection by making it crystal clear the choice is simply part of his diabolical plot to bag the elephant—aka, get the girl. "Women always fall for that sentimental crap."

I knew otherwise, though. I knew my vodka-drinking, pistachio-eating buddy ached to be in love. To have someone he could create bittersweet memories with. It must have been hard wearing that mask all these years, alone.

A few days later, my dad is released from the hospital. Although they won't know for at least another six months if the valve replacements are truly successful, the doctors seem optimistic. It appears that he's out of any real danger and should be okay.

After hiring a nurse to be with him during the final stage of his rehabilitation, I book my flight to return to Chicago. I have been in Florida for seven weeks now and have learned how to tolerate bad Jewish drivers and how to do my own laundry. I've also seen every episode of *The Golden Girls* ever made. I was proud of my father's son, and I knew my own kids were proud of their dad. But now it was time to return home. Before I leave, however, I have to go say good-bye.

CHAPTER 38

I haven't been back to her grave since the day of the funeral. As I look down at the rectangular patch of fresh black dirt, I swear to God I can still see her bright, sparkly blue eyes. I'll miss so many things about her, including how with the passing of every year she began wearing her pants higher and higher.

I begin circling the grave. This box in the earth is her new home. She would have been seventy the next month.

As I circle her grave for the sixty-ninth and final time, I can't believe I'll never be able to touch her again. Never be able to hug her. Never be able to hear her voice. I reach into my pocket for my cell phone and dial 847-863-0009. After three rings, I hear it.

"This is Gloria. I'm not in right now. Please leave a message. Beep."

So I do. Standing beside her rectangular patch of fresh black dirt, I speak into the phone as I look up at the clouds. “I love you, Mom. Bye.”

CHAPTER 39

That night I meet my dad's caretaker and she seems nice. My dad whispers, "Go hide your mother's jewelry."

He starts to cry. He has mastered the ability to make you feel guilty at any time, day or night, for just about anything. I never held him in my arms like this before. Like a child. I rub his back and tell him everything is going to be all right. I can smell the cologne my mom always told him he thought he needed too much of. I love my dad, and the best part about that fact is that he knows it.

I see him watching me from the window as I back out of the driveway. Before the last tire rolls over the curb, I notice him holding up a poster board under his chin—the homemade kind Girl Scouts make when they're selling lemonade on the corner. At first I can't make out what it says. Eventually I do. In big red letters, he's written, Don't Forget To Take I-95. LESS TRAFFIC!

I put my hand to my lips and blow him a kiss good-bye.

You can determine a lot about a person by how they act immediately after a plane lands. There are those with places to be and people to see and then there are the other folks. The ones with an eternity and a day on their hands. I duck, dart, and dodge my way off, apologizing for my rudeness.

There stands my world. My twins look the same, but I swear Sage seems to have grown taller. And Andi is more beautiful than I even remember. They're all in their pj's. We hug and touch and kiss long enough to allow my suitcases to make two spins around the carousel. Eventually we break apart and start for the exit. But before I'm allowed to leave, Sage hands me a paper bag and smiles. I think even his teeth got bigger. Inside this Target bag are my pajamas. My youngest son orders me to go change into them. I put my bag down and head for the closest men's room along the corridor.

CHAPTER 40

If you really want to practice your reading, go away for eight weeks and come back to eight weeks' worth of mail. Being back was wonderful. And a relief. And odd. Two months earlier, I left Chicago with two parents. Now I return having only one. What you realize after you lose a parent is just how much you love being a parent. How you can't possibly imagine life without these pocket people sleeping in the rooms next to you. How all those things you once complained about—getting up in the middle of the night for the fifth time or running out to buy more diapers or sitting for three hours inside an airless gymnasium at a dance recital watching four-year-olds caroming into each other—you would pay a lifetime of salary to do all over again. And how you promise yourself you will now do everything not to miss anything.

For the first time in the history of my tutoring career, I am about to share the stage with another tutor—actually *two* other tutors. It's my first day back, and after picking up Isabella and Oliver from school, we head directly downtown to the literacy center. Although I've heard all about their progress, I can't wait to see it up close. After receiving a hero's welcome, accessorized with hugs, handshakes, and a two-hour-old carrot cake Gail baked, I take a seat in the gallery next to Charles and get ready for the floor show. Man, Charles smells good enough to take to the drive-in.

Aunt June and Marilyn, the stern but sweet office manager, decide to join today's session. They take the two chairs in front to the right. Watching Isabella and Oliver play off each other is a thing of beauty. Their timing is as good as a professional comedy team's. He's her Costello; she's his Abbott. But what I notice most is how the room cannot take their eyes off them. These strangers have fallen hard for my twins. And even though it is quite evident Isabella and Oliver have more than four hundred years' worth of adulthood resting in the palm of their hands, you can tell they respect and honor this bestowed affection. Although not yet thirteen, each fully understands the magnitude of what has happened and is happening inside this room.

The class votes on their favorite song selection. The winner's song will be written on the board again, re-dissected, and replayed on Belly's iPod. An encore presentation. Everyone hopes that in the end Aunt June Porter will be persuaded to join the group as they dance around the room. The ballots are counted and the champion is crowned. It's a landslide: "Sweep

Around Your Own Front Door" is the victor. Anne Marie rises from her chair, takes a slurp from her Big Gulp, and curtsies to the crowd.

The two pint-size tutors break apart from one another and take their positions. Oliver remains at the blackboard in the front of the classroom, and Isabella gracefully moves to the second blackboard recently installed in the rear. Simultaneously they begin writing, their pieces of chalk perfectly harmonized. And then, like tenured teachers, they take their students on a journey through the lyrics step-by-step. It's incredible to watch. Circling certain words, separating syllables, and conquering sentences. Alternating from student to student to student. Nobody raises their hand, yet there's complete order.

When the final line is read, the walls erupt. Anne Marie gives another royal curtsy. Isabella rejoins Oliver at the front of the room and they high-five each other. Maybe I had been wrong at the airport. They do look taller. Isabella reaches in her pocket and pulls out her iPod.

"Shhh. Everybody quiet. Get ready, it's about to start," says Edna.

"Shut the f— up," adds Michael.

"What did you just say?" Marilyn asks as she moves toward Michael.

"Sorry . . . *Please* shut the f— up!"

Even Marilyn can't suppress a smirk. Joining the others, she starts laughing as she waves him off and returns to her seat. Before the first sound erupts from the speaker, they're up out of their chairs. It's like *Fame*, only older.

Bad voices and all, it's an exhibit worth paying to see. My

kids holding hands and dancing with these eight men and women makes me smile so hard it hurts. They would never have been privileged to meet these exceptional people if it weren't for this nonjudgmental sanctuary where people simply root for you.

What makes me laugh, however, is when I see Melvin approach Aunt June Porter like he's back at his eighth grade Valentine's Day dance. He extends his hand gently and gestures for Aunt June to join him. Like a shy schoolgirl, she grins at Marilyn, pulls herself out from her seat, fixes her hair without touching it, and takes Melvin's hand.

"Look, look everybody," begs Elvira. "Miss Porter's dancing, Miss Porter's dancing."

And she is. Slowly at first, but in time, this eighty-something great-grandma brushes her date to the side and begins seductively moving every single part of her body. She swivels up and down like a stubborn cork climbing out of a wine bottle.

After a quick bathroom, water, and cigarette break, we return to conquer the second item on today's syllabus. Everyone takes out his or her copy of the book they selected right before my sudden departure. It's time to continue onward with *Black Beauty*. They all seem so excited I begin to wonder what is in that drinking fountain. They can barely stay in their seats.

Although I knew it would take some work, I had hoped we could finish the entire book by the end of the summer. I knew they started while I was gone, but I had no idea how far they had gotten. Turns out that was the cause for all the excitement. With the help of Aunt June arranging for the center to stay open later during the week and on Saturdays, Isabella and Oliver started holding more sessions. Andi would drop them off with care packages of coffee and juices and every item from the Hostess aisle at the grocery store, including, but not limited to, HoHos, Ding Dongs, Twinkies, Suzy Q's, Donettes, Zingers, and Snoballs. Anne Marie was in non-nutritious heaven. I'm not sure if it was the caffeine or the perpetual sugar rush, but somehow they managed to land on page 221 this very evening—the page right before the page with the words *The End* branded at the bottom. I don't know how they did it; they just did.

The surprise, kept tightly gift-wrapped, was that they waited for me. They could have finished the week before, but they didn't. They chose to wait until I got back. And according to the whole group, the loudest voice calling for it was none other than Michael.

"Of course we gotta f—in' wait for him. He's our f—in' tutor." Sometimes certain words have such a sweetness to them!

Like dutiful chaperones, Oliver and Isabella come to get me from my chair. Each taking one of my hands, they escort me to the front of the room. On the desk sits my copy of *Black Beauty,* folded to the final page. Although there are no drums, you can still hear them roll. As if reciting the Pledge of Allegiance, together my eight students stand and read aloud in unison. Each word is spoken as though it's the single most important word ever created. And even though their hands are not resting over their hearts, I feel like all their hearts are now resting in my hands.

In the afternoon I was put into a low park chair and brought to the door. Miss Ellen was going to try me, and Green went with her. I soon found that she was a good driver, and she seemed pleased with my paces. I heard Joe telling her about me, and that he was sure I was Squire Gordon's old Black Beauty.

When we returned the other sisters came out to hear how I behaved myself. She told them what she had just heard, and said:

"I shall certainly write to Mrs. Gordon, and tell her that her favorite horse has come to us. How pleased she will be!"

After this I was driven every day for a week or so, and as I appeared to be quite safe, Miss Lavinia at last ventured out in the small close carriage. After this it was quite decided to keep me and call me my old name of "Black Beauty."

I have now lived in this happy place for a whole year. Joe is the best and kindest of grooms. My work is easy and pleasant, and I feel my strength and spirits all coming back again. Mr. Thoroughgood said to Joe the other day:

"In your place he will last till he is twenty years old—perhaps more."

Willie always speaks to me when he can, and treats me as his special friend. My ladies have promised that I shall never be sold, and so I have nothing to fear; and here my story ends. My troubles are all over, and I am at home; and often before I am quite awake, I fancy I am still in the orchard at Birtwick, standing with my old friends under the apple trees.

THE END

CHAPTER 41

Two weeks ago Isabella celebrated her Bat Mitzvah and Oliver his Bar Mitzvah. With twins, the plural, B'nai Mitzvah is used. I don't know who came up with the idea that at age thirteen a boy miraculously turns into a man. I'm forty-eight years old and still waiting for that transformation to take effect. But anyone who is a parent knows exactly what we were feeling sitting in the audience of the temple that morning watching our babies stand before God reading from the Torah. Nobody could ever prepare you for this: namely, that you could ever be capable of loving something so much. From the first moment I laid eyes on them, I knew I was changed forever.

A few weeks earlier, this guy wearing an official-looking nametag came by our house looking for us to complete the

U.S. Census Application. As we sat at my kitchen table, Todd removed the sharpened pencil from behind his ear and started asking the questions on the form and recording my answers. My profession? Lawyer. How many adults in the home? Two. Any other people residing in the household? Three. Names? Isabella, Oliver, and Sage. After jotting down their names, Todd asked what their relationship to me was. As the words daughter and son left my lips, for some reason I heard them like I never had before. She is my daughter and they are my sons. And I'm not a lawyer. I'm their dad. That's my job! I can't believe how fast it's all going by.

A requirement for a child celebrating a Bat or Bar Mitzvah is for her or him to complete a mitzvah project. In Hebrew, the word *mitzvah* means "a good deed performed out of religious duty." In other words, doing something nice for someone else simply for the sake of doing it. Some teens work at a soup kitchen on a few Saturdays. Others visit hospitals or nursing homes a couple of times. Isabella and Oliver unintentionally and suddenly became involved in another kind of project. Here's an excerpt from the speech Oliver gave to the congregation at the conclusion of the service, in which he describes what his mitzvah project meant to him.

> My mitzvah project was helping adults who can't read. I wasn't planning on making this my project. I didn't choose it. I guess my grandma chose it for me. There are people at the center in their thirties and forties. There's this one man who's even almost seventy. He smells really great, though. They never learned how to read

before. Why being there is so special for me is because a few years ago, I had a hard time learning to read. Everybody was trying to help me, but I just couldn't do it. It was scary sitting in class every day praying that the teacher wouldn't call on me because I didn't want to be embarrassed. I remember wondering why other kids knew how to read and I didn't. I felt really stupid. We're not allowed to use that word at the literacy center.

Today, I'm a pretty good reader. But I can't imagine what it would be like not to have my parents or people like my teachers who helped me. I mean, my mom and dad were sometimes a giant pain in the you-know-what about learning my flash cards or getting my pennies every night, but I know it's because they love me. And being at the literacy center helping Harold or Gail sound out words feels truly amazing. It was kind of like I was sharing something I got that they never did. And when we all finished *Black Beauty*, it was better than when I won that big trophy when I played on the Orioles. My parents always tell me how important education is. Now I see that it's true. I see how not having it can make such a difference and how Melvin takes two different buses and a train just to come to have a chance to learn how to read so he can get a better job to help his family. Every time I leave there, I feel really happy inside my heart

Thank you.

Jewish protocol dictates that you're not supposed to clap and whistle and scream at the top of your bloody lungs after someone speaks in the synagogue. Fortunately, on this particular Saturday morning, the eight students sitting in the third row wearing their Sunday best had never heard about that rule. They gave Oliver a standing ovation.

Turns out, whether sitting in a temple, a church, a diner, or a downtown classroom, we're all here to teach each other something. Sometimes, we just have to get our heads out of the clouds.

EPILOGUE

A few weeks ago, Charles vanished and stopped coming to the literacy center. His phone had been disconnected, and nobody knew where he was. After tracking down one of his cousins, I finally found Charles. The look in his eyes when he opened his door and saw me standing there was something I will never forget. He was depressed because he had lost his part-time job and things weren't going so well for him. His fancy suit and shiny shoes had been replaced by shorts, a T-shirt, and flip-flops. And the Charles sparkle that made him the center's designated motivational speaker had also disappeared.

Charles now stays in a type of government-funded senior citizens building that coincidentally is about ten blocks from where my family and I live. The unit he lives in is a few inches bigger than the box his former shiny shoes came in. And every parcel of wall is covered with framed pictures of Charles and different people he has met over the years. Athletes, entertainers, lots and lots of women. There's Charles posing with first lady Barbara Bush (he lived in Midland, Texas, at the time) and one with him and Oprah's boyfriend, Stedman. There's a shelf filled with books he can't read and a set of old golf clubs and a tennis racket he hasn't used in a long time.

Charles is someone who certainly deserves more, and at sixty-three, he still dreams. His dream was always to write screenplays. A few years ago, he got a job at a place that produced industrial films that corporations use for their training sessions or public service announcements. He was doing great. They wanted to promote him to a position where he would proofread scripts. That's the day he left and never came back.

After we talked together for an hour or so, I convinced him to go grab a bite to eat with me. We walked to a place on the corner and sat at the counter. I know it sounds cornier than a bad soap opera, but we ordered one hot dog and one hamburger and cut each down the middle. The following day, Charles returned to Literacy Chicago and is now back in rare form, more motivated than ever.

We all get down at times. Doctors, lawyers, Indian chiefs. Even an eloquent gentleman trying to learn how to read. But I can see it in his smile that the more words Charles continues to "own," the higher his dreams climb.

We don't often concern ourselves with societal injustices unless and until we find them relevant inside our own world. Similar to any malignant growth, low literacy levels reside in all neighborhoods. With modern medical advancement, people live longer. Those who can't read will continue to struggle harder, never reaching their true potential. As a nation, we constantly complain about the increasing degree of criminal behavior on our streets. But when someone is unable to read and can't find work, they are frequently forced to turn toward other means of "employment."

We must begin attacking literacy issues at the top of the food chain. Adults! The statistics are crystal clear: Households where moms and dads or the care provider are low-level readers are much more likely to produce sons and daughters who are equally educationally deficient. We are obligated to help each other become better. One hour each week. That's the challenge. Find a tutoring facility in your community by going to www.nationalliteracydirectory.org, click the box "I want to Volunteer at a Program," and enter your zip code. It's as easy as that. And who knows? The stranger you help for sixty minutes a week may someday give your own child a standing ovation.

AKNOWLEDGMENTS

I had no idea of the length and breadth of commitment this book would require of me in writing it. The phrase "it takes a village" is used too often, but not in this case. Without the love and reinforcement from Andi, Isabella, Oliver, and Sage, page one could never have been written. Fairy tales really do come true. I love you wildly my Wild Thornberrys.

But it wasn't just my family who provided the nourishment for this achievement. There were other sources of support, some coming from complete strangers.

Like Bruce, the manager at Starbucks on the concourse level of the courthouse who religiously guarded my corner table where I wrote nearly half of this book. And Tanya, the charming waitress at Giordano's Pizza Parlor who always had my cup of minestrone soup and glass of Diet Coke with two wedges of lemon waiting for every Thursday afternoon's writing session before I even took off my suit coat. And Marilyn, the stern but sweet office manager at Literacy Chicago who never failed to make sure my classroom was properly outfitted with multicolored Sharpies and a freshly cleaned eraser. And, of course, every student I have ever had the privilege of standing before sounding out together our A-E-I-O-Us and sometimes Ys. (That's for you, Ms. Cheri!)

Sincerest thanks to Aunt June Porter, too, my adopted grandmother, mentor, therapist, and friend. I am truly different inside because of you.

After finishing *Hot Dogs & Hamburgers*, I submitted the manuscript to more than 150 literary agents. Not a single response. In early January of this year, Andi came up with the brainstorm of forwarding it to "that guy who cowrote *The Last Lecture*. He seems like a really good person."

After tracking down an email address for him, I sent Jeffrey Zaslow a note. The best-selling author had just begun his book-signing tour for his newest release, *The Magic Room*. And yet, inside of forty-eight hours, I received a response. Finally, someone had noticed. He heard the voice of a stranger and offered advice, direction, and hope. He explained how hard this endeavor would be. How agents and publishing companies want clients with a "platform." How, frankly, a lawyer from Chicago is a harder sell. But he said that I had talent and persistence and he could see my book making something happen in the fields of literacy and learning differences. He closed by telling me my family is lucky to have such a loving husband and father. I am the lucky one.

I want to recognize Mr. Zaslow as someone I never officially met but who extended himself to me as if we had known each other since summer camp. He tragically passed away on February 10, 2012, but his words surprised and revived me. As a result of his encouraging message, I drew energy and courage to continue pursuing the publication of our story.

Thanks to Greenleaf Book Group who took a chance when nobody else would. To Neil Gonzalez, the talented designer who created a cover and interior pages that greatly enhanced the book. And to my brilliant lead editor, Linda O'Doughda, whose guidance and brutal (but always loving) honesty forced this writer to become an author.

Finally, a special thank-you to my mom. I miss you every day, and I'd give anything to hear that Gloria laugh one more time.

ABOUT THE AUTHOR

Rob and his wife, Andi, have twins, Isabella and Oliver, and their younger brother, future NFL star Sage. Rob is the founder of Abogados America, a small law firm in Chicago that specializes in representing the Hispanic community, which faces an array of legal injustices.

"My Spanish-speaking clients are a lot like adults fighting illiteracy. Society tends to judge both before all the evidence is in." Rob's hope is that *Hot Dogs & Hamburgers* will bring an awareness of adult low literacy and slow that judging process down.